T0327599

A Guide to Business Statistics

A Guide to Business Statistics

David M. McEvoy

Registered Office
John Wiley & Sons, Inc., 111 River Street, Hoboken, NJ 07030, USA

Editorial Office
111 River Street, Hoboken, NJ 07030, USA

For details of our global editorial offices, customer services, and more information about Wiley products visit us at www.wiley.com.

Wiley also publishes its books in a variety of electronic formats and by print-on-demand. Some content that appears in standard print versions of this book may not be available in other formats.

Library of Congress Cataloguing-in-Publication Data:

Names: McEvoy, David M. (David Michael), author.
Title: A guide to business statistics / by David M. McEvoy.
Description: Hoboken, NJ : John Wiley & Sons, Inc., 2018. | Includes
    bibliographical references and index. |
Identifiers: LCCN 2017051197 (print) | LCCN 2017054561 (ebook) | ISBN
    9781119138365 (pdf) | ISBN 9781119138372 (epub) | ISBN 9781119138358 (pbk.)
Subjects: LCSH: Commercial statistics.
Classification: LCC HF1017 (ebook) | LCC HF1017 .M37 2018 (print) | DDC
    519.5–dc23
LC record available at https://lccn.loc.gov/2017051197

Cover Design: Wiley
Cover Image: Derivative of "Rock Climbing in Joshua Tree National Park" by Contributor7001 is licensed under CC BY-SA

Printed in the United States of America

Set in 10/12pt WarnockPro by SPi Global, Chennai, India

10 9 8 7 6 5 4 3 2 1

Dedicated to my students who managed to stay awake during class, and to my family who are clearly a few standard deviations above the mean: Marta, Leo, Sofia, and Oscar

Contents

Preface   *xiii*

1   **Types of Data**   *1*
1.1   Categorical Data   *2*
1.2   Numerical Data   *3*
1.3   Level of Measurement   *4*
1.4   Cross-Sectional, Time-Series, and Panel Data   *5*
1.5   Summary   *7*

2   **Populations and Samples**   *9*
2.1   What is the Population of Interest?   *10*
2.2   How to Sample From a Population?   *11*
2.2.1   Simple Random Sampling   *11*
2.2.2   Stratified Sampling   *14*
2.2.3   Other Methods   *15*
2.3   Getting the Data   *16*
2.4   Summary   *17*

3   **Descriptive Statistics**   *19*
3.1   Measures of Central Tendency   *20*
3.1.1   The Mean   *20*
3.1.2   The Median   *23*
3.1.3   The Mode   *24*
3.2   Measures of Variability   *24*
3.2.1   Variance and Standard Deviation   *24*
3.3   The Shape   *26*
3.4   Summary   *28*
      Technical Appendix   *29*

4   Probability *31*
4.1   Simple Probabilities *32*
4.1.1   When to Add Probabilities Together *34*
4.1.2   When to Find Intersections *36*
4.2   Empirical Probabilities *37*
4.3   Conditional Probabilities *39*
4.4   Summary *41*
         Technical Appendix *42*

5   The Normal Distribution *43*
5.1   The Bell Shape *43*
5.2   The Empirical Rule *44*
5.3   Standard Normal Distribution *46*
5.3.1   Probabilities with Continuous Distributions *48*
5.3.2   Verifying the Empirical Rule Using the z-table *48*
5.4   Normal Approximations *48*
5.4.1   Mean *49*
5.4.2   Standard deviation *49*
5.4.3   Shape *50*
5.5   Summary *51*
         Technical Appendix *52*

6   Sampling Distributions *55*
6.1   Defining a Sampling Distribution *55*
6.2   The Importance of Sampling Distributions *56*
6.3   An Example of a Sampling Distribution *57*
6.4   Characteristics of a Sampling Distribution of a Mean *61*
6.4.1   The Mean *61*
6.4.2   The Shape *62*
6.4.3   The Standard Deviation *64*
6.4.4   Finding Probabilities With a Sampling Distribution *65*
6.5   Sampling Distribution of a Proportion *67*
6.5.1   The Mean *68*
6.5.2   The Shape *68*
6.5.3   The Standard Deviation *68*
6.6   Summary *70*
         Technical Appendix *71*

7   Confidence Intervals *73*
7.1   Confidence Intervals for Means *74*
7.1.1   The Characteristics of the Sampling Distribution *75*
7.1.2   Confidence Intervals Using the z-Distribution *76*
7.1.3   Confidence Intervals Using the t-Distribution *78*

7.2   Confidence Intervals for Proportions   *80*
7.3   Sample Size and the Width of Confidence Intervals   *81*
7.4   Comparing Two Proportions From the Same Poll   *82*
7.5   Summary   *84*
         Technical Appendix   *85*

8   **Hypothesis Tests of a Population Mean**   *89*
8.1   Two-Tail Hypothesis Test of a Mean   *90*
8.1.1   A Single Sample from a Population   *90*
8.1.2   Setting Up the Null and Alternative Hypothesis   *92*
8.1.3   Decisions and Errors   *92*
8.1.4   Rejection Regions and Conclusions   *94*
8.1.5   Changing the Level of Significance   *95*
8.2   One-Tail Hypothesis Test of a Mean   *97*
8.2.1   Setting Up the Null and Alternative Hypotheses   *97*
8.2.2   Rejection Regions and Conclusions   *98*
8.3   *p*-Value Approach to Hypothesis Tests   *99*
8.3.1   One-Tail Tests   *99*
8.3.2   Two-tail tests   *100*
8.4   Summary   *100*
         Technical Appendix   *101*

9   **Hypothesis Tests of Categorical Data**   *103*
9.1   Two-Tail Hypothesis Test of a Proportion   *104*
9.1.1   A Single Sample from a Population   *104*
9.1.2   Rejection Regions and Conclusions   *106*
9.2   One-Tail Hypothesis Test of a Proportion   *107*
9.3   Using *p*-Values   *108*
9.3.1   One-Tail Tests Using the *p*-Value   *108*
9.3.2   Two-Tail Tests Using the *p*-Value   *108*
9.4   Chi-Square Tests   *109*
9.4.1   The Data in a Contingency Table   *109*
9.4.2   Chi-Square Test of Goodness of Fit   *111*
9.5   Summary   *114*
         Technical Appendix   *115*

10   **Hypothesis Tests Comparing Two Parameters**   *117*
10.1   The Approach in this Chapter   *118*
10.2   Hypothesis Tests of Two Means   *118*
10.2.1   The Null and Alternative Hypothesis   *118*
10.2.2   *t*-Test Assuming Equal Variances   *121*
10.2.3   *t*-Test Assuming Unequal Variances   *122*
10.2.4   One-Tail Hypothesis Tests of Two Means   *124*

10.2.5   A Note on Hypothesis Tests Using Paired Observations   *124*
10.3   Hypothesis Tests of Two Variances   *126*
10.4   Hypothesis Tests of Two Proportions   *128*
10.5   Summary   *130*
          Technical Appendix   *131*

11   **Simple Linear Regression**   *133*
11.1   The Population Regression Model   *134*
11.2   A Look at the Data   *135*
11.3   Ordinary Least Squares (OLS)   *137*
11.4   The Distribution of b_0 and b_1 *139*
11.5   Tests of Significance   *140*
11.6   Goodness of Fit   *142*
11.7   Checking for Violations of the Assumptions   *143*
11.7.1   The Normality Assumption   *143*
11.7.2   The Constant Variance Assumption   *144*
11.8   Summary   *146*
          Technical Appendix   *147*

12   **Multiple Regression**   *149*
12.1   Population Regression Model   *149*
12.2   The Data   *150*
12.3   Sample Regression Function   *151*
12.4   Interpreting the Estimates   *152*
12.4.1   Attendance   *153*
12.4.2   SAT   *153*
12.4.3   Hours Studying   *153*
12.4.4   Logic Test   *153*
12.4.5   Female   *153*
12.4.6   Senior   *154*
12.5   Prediction   *154*
12.6   Tests of Significance   *154*
12.6.1   Joint Hypothesis Test   *155*
12.7   Goodness of Fit   *156*
12.8   Multicollinearity   *157*
12.8.1   Variance Inflation Factor (VIF)   *157*
12.8.2   An Example of Violating the Assumption of no
          Multicollinearity   *159*
12.9   Summary   *162*
          Technical Appendix   *163*

13   **More Topics in Regression**   *165*

13.1   Hypothesis Tests Comparing Two Means With Regression   *165*

13.2   Hypothesis Tests Comparing More Than Two Means (ANOVA)   *168*

13.3   Interacting Variables   *170*

13.3.1   Gender Differences in Starting Wages   *171*

13.3.2   Gender Differences in Wage Increase from Experience   *172*

13.4   Nonlinearities   *173*

13.5   Time-Series Analysis   *175*

13.6   Summary   *177*

Index   *179*

Preface

When the Boston Red Sox traded Babe Ruth to the New York Yankees in 1919, they were one of the most successful baseball teams in history. At that time, the Red Sox held five World Series titles, with the most recent in 1918. That trade would start an 86-year dry spell for the Red Sox, during which they would not win a single national title. That trade would start what baseball fans know as the *Curse of the Bambino*. The Curse supposedly made Johnny Pesky hesitate at shortstop in a routine throw home in game seven of the 1946 World Series. The Curse showed up when Bob Stanley threw a wild pitch in game six of the 1986 World Series that let the tying run in, and stayed to see Bill Buckner let a ground ball pass between his legs at first base. The Red Sox finally broke the curse in 2004 beating the St. Louis Cardinals. How did the Boston Red Sox break the *Curse of the Bambino*? Statistics.

Ok, perhaps attributing the Red Sox's 2004 title and the two that followed entirely to statistics is a bit of a reach. Statistics, however, played a role. In 2002, Theo Epstein was hired as the general manager (GM) for the Red Sox. He was the youngest GM in the history of major league baseball. Epstein relied heavily on statistics when building team rosters and making managerial decisions. He was an early adopter of what is called *sabermetrics* – which is a statistical analysis of baseball. His approach focused on utilizing undervalued players, including those who were on the verge of leaving the game because no other team would sign them. The movement was away from flashy players with big risks and big rewards to the more inconspicuous workhorses. It worked. Of course, it is possible that Theo Epstein and the Boston Red Sox just got lucky. Consider, however, that Theo Epstein was hired as the President of Baseball Operations for the Chicago Cubs in 2011. In 2016, the Cubs would win their first World Series in 108 years. It would end yet another curse – the *Curse of the Billy Goat* – that prevented the Cubs from winning for 71 years. Again, statistics.

Addressing Two Challenges

Over the past dozen years, I have taught courses in business statistics to thousands of undergraduate students. As an instructor, one of the challenges with teaching statistics is trying to convince students that the material is important. I usually take two approaches. The first is to persuade students that they need to understand statistics as *consumers* of information. We are bombarded with information every single day and it is coming at us from every direction. Our news sources and social media platforms are crawling with statistics. On a Monday, I may learn that coffee is good for me and by Wednesday it is now the kiss of death. In the 1980s, eggs were cholesterol-filled heart attack triggers and today they are considered the perfect food. On any given day, I can read about studies that tell me how to live longer, run faster, have more energy, make more money, be a better parent, and be happier. These types of studies all rely on statistics. Some of the information we get is from scientific studies – those that rely on the scientific method – but other information is very ad hoc. Understanding what the statistics tell us, how they are calculated, and the samples they are derived from is key to processing all of the information we consume. Understanding statistics can help you pick out the nuggets of useful information from the big mess of the modern information age.

The other approach I take in trying to convey the importance of statistics is to appeal to the students as *producers* of information. It is probably safe to assume that most people do not enjoy cranking through formulas and pouring over spreadsheets of data. However, everyone is interested in something. Perhaps you are interested in investing in the stock market and you need to decide which firms to invest in. Maybe you need to convince your boss which social media platform to advertise on. Maybe you need to persuade your parents that spending a semester studying abroad is a useful experience. The point is that everyone has interesting questions, and answering those questions usually requires some form of data analysis. Just having data is not enough, you need to know how to release its secrets.

The second challenge with teaching statistics is that, in my experience, many students dread the thought of the subject, and often walk through the door the first day of class already resigned to the idea that they will hate it. Typically, students believe that they will dislike statistics because they consider the subject too hard, or it requires too much math. Adding to the list of students' fears and concerns is the fact that most of the materials created for undergraduate courses in business statistics try to accomplish too many things and as a result are overwhelming. Textbooks try to balance a mix of theory, intuition, formulas, case studies, datasets, applets, problem sets, and the practical use of particular software programs. All of these are important objectives, but when blended together each tends to get crowded out. In my experience, students use their statistics textbooks as reference guides to look up formulas or functions, but in the process miss the fundamental concepts and intuition.

The objective of this book is to try help ease both of these challenges. The goal of each chapter is to first motivate a particular section of business statistics and then walk through the concepts in an intuitive fashion. The book is driven by examples and many of the examples span over multiple chapters. The book was written with a goal of removing many of the distractions students encounter in their statistics textbooks. Mathematical formulas and much of the notation are relegated to technical appendices at the end of each chapter. There are no online applets, data downloads, or breakout case studies. The prose is written so that it is hopefully inviting to students with different backgrounds and experiences. The focus is more on developing intuition and understanding the fundamentals than it is on being a comprehensive catalog of statistical tests.

How to Use This Book

This book is not designed to be used as a primary source of information for an undergraduate statistics course. It does not cover every figure, statistic, or hypothesis test you will find in a comprehensive textbook. It is meant to be a supplement to a more detailed textbook and/or a set of lecture notes. It should be thought of as a companion guide with the goal of helping students get a better grasp on the fundamentals. In this way, the primary textbook serves as the comprehensive catalog of information and, perhaps, the source of assessment materials, while *A Guide to Business Statistics* serves as the source for students to strengthen their intuition about the concepts and their applicability. However, for classes in which the instructor provides all the required technical details in the lecture notes and does not rely on a textbook to assign problems, homework, or practice datasets, *A Guide to Business Statistics* can serve as a primary textbook. In these cases, students will read the book to complement the material covered in lecture with the goal of providing an intuitive and example-driven approach to better understand the material. This book maintains the level of rigor of a standard textbook in business statistics, but with a more streamlined approach and accessible explanation of the material.

It is not surprising that most students do not read their undergraduate statistics textbooks in a linear fashion. If anything, they tend to skim through the pages in search for formulas, tables, or functions. The chapters in most statistics textbooks are very difficult to read from start to finish, and to be fair they are not designed for that approach. This book is designed to be easy to read and, most importantly, concise. Students should open a chapter and read it from start to finish and at the end have a good understanding of the core concepts for that section. The chapters include examples, simple tables and figures, and a technical appendix with the formulas. At the end of each chapter (before the appendix), the key elements are reinforced in a brief summary paragraph. To maintain its readability in a linear fashion, it purposefully avoids problem sets, animations, video clips, and interactive materials.

Another important distinction between standard textbooks and *A Guide to Business Statistics* is the treatment of statistical software programs. Textbooks are increasingly focused on how to better integrate statistics software (e.g., Excel, SPSS, and Minitab) with the course material. This is important because students should be able to use technology to analyze data and produce statistical output. However, while many students are capable of running a statistical test in a program like Excel, there is often a lack of general understanding regarding the underlying concepts and interpretations of the results. For example, most students can successfully create a confidence interval if provided a dataset. Fewer students can correctly interpret a confidence interval, and even fewer can still explain the theorems those interpretations are grounded in. I would argue that understanding the underlying concepts in statistics is more important than learning how to use a certain software package to generate statistical output. The technology is going to change, but the concepts and theorems that are fundamental to statistics are not tied to specific platforms. This book does contain references to statistical functions in Excel, especially in the chapters on regression analysis. Software programs like Excel are absolutely required for any analysis of large datasets. The point of this book, however, is not to develop a student's skill set in any particular software program. Running a regression in Excel is just as easy as in SPSS or Minitab. The point, rather, is to help interpret the output that is produced by *any* software program.

The trajectory of the chapters follows most of the standard textbooks in business statistics. The coverage of the material in each chapter is designed to be more "narrow and deep" rather than "broad and shallow." That said, in my experience, all of the key materials required in a first and second course in undergraduate business statistics are covered in this book. The first part of the book is concentrated on how we collect and describe data (Chapters 1–6) and the second half is focused on how to use sample data to make inferences about things we do not know about a population of interest (Chapters 7–13). The chapters on inferential statistics focus on parametric tests – those that assume that the data follow a particular type of distribution. These are the most common tests in business and other social sciences. The final three chapters of the book cover linear regression techniques.

Target Audience

This book should serve as a useful guide for all undergraduate statistics students in business and economics, regardless of the specific primary textbook (if any) they are using in their course. Almost all business and economics majors are required to complete a course in statistics, and many 4-year business programs require two courses as part of the major. In addition, most 2-year colleges offer an introductory course in statistics. When two courses are required, it is often the case that the same primary textbook is used in both courses. *A Guide to Business Statistics* is geared to students taking both their first and second courses in statistics. The first course is typically taken as a freshman or sophomore and the second as a junior or senior. The book, therefore, should prove useful over all four undergraduate years.

Although the book is geared toward students in higher education, it may be a helpful resource to faculty and instructors who have been away from statistics for some time. It can serve as a concise "refresher" resource for teachers and practitioners.

1

Types of Data

Steven Wright once joked that "42.7% of all statistics are made up on the spot."[1] One reason that his quip is effective is because there are good reasons to be suspicious of many of the statistics we encounter every day. Statistics are often reported as hard facts that cannot be argued with. This is not so. Statistics, and the data that the statistics are derived from, are generated by humans. Humans are not infallible and neither are the numbers reported from analyzing the data. As consumers of information, sometimes the statistics we encounter are just simply wrong or even nonsensical. There are examples of peer-reviewed publications reporting 200% reductions in some metric. Even reductions of 12,000% have been reported.[2] Without even glancing at the data analyzed in these studies, we know that such statistics are nonsense. You cannot decrease anything by more than 100%. Once you lose 100% of stuff, you are out of stuff. We tend to believe assertions when they are based on data. The problem is that we often do not look carefully at what type of data is being analyzed, how the data were gathered, and whether the results are valid. To be an active and informed citizen, you need to understand a bit about how statistics are generated and what they can tell us. It all starts with understanding the type of data being analyzed, which is the focus of this first chapter.

In the broadest terms, *statistics* is the science of collecting, analyzing, and interpreting data. One branch of statistics is concerned with how to describe and present data in useful ways (*descriptive statistics*) and the other branch is concerned with how to use samples of data to draw conclusions about unknown characteristics of a larger population (*inferential statistics*). In either case, the starting point is understanding a bit about data. Often, when students hear the term data or data analysis, they picture some geek crunching through endless columns of numbers in search for answers. The truth is that data are simply organized *information*. Data does not have to be numeric, and not all numeric

---

1 He also has a line that "five out of four people have trouble with fractions."
2 Pollack, L. and H. Weiss. (1984) "Communication satellites: Countdown for intelsat VI." Science 223(4636):553.

A Guide to Business Statistics, First Edition. David M. McEvoy.
© 2018 John Wiley & Sons, Inc. Published 2018 by John Wiley & Sons, Inc.

data can be treated the same way. One great thing about the modern state of technology and connectivity is that we have access to incredible amounts of interesting, and often peculiar, datasets. For example, you can read the last words of every executed criminal in the state of Texas since 1982.[3] Or, if you think that is too morbid, you may be interested in the location, speed, age, and height of amusement park rollercoasters found all over the world.[4] Perhaps, you want to rank every character on the Simpsons by the number of words they spoke between season 1 and season 26.[5] The point is that there is so much data available to the public that the possibilities are endless. If you want to get weird, get weird.[6] You can let your imagination lead you to data, but let this book guide you on how to analyze it.

The important point is to recognize what type of data you are working with because that will dictate the way you analyze it. In this chapter, we consider the taxonomy of different data types. To begin, all data can be broadly classified as either *categorical* or *numerical*.

1.1 Categorical Data

Categorical data (also called *qualitative data*) have values described by words rather than numbers. Examples include gender, occupation, major, and location. Often, categorical data are represented with *codes* to make it easier to manage and manipulate. For example, a dataset that includes college majors may convert accounting = 1, economics = 2, and marketing = 3. The important distinction between these codes and numeric data is that the codes typically do not convey a ranking, they are just a way to organize categorical data. When data can be classified by two categories, we call that *binary* data. Examples include gender in which female = 1 and male = 0. Even when data have more than two categories, the qualitative data can often be represented in binary form. As an example, consider the three majors: accounting, economics, and marketing. If each observation in a dataset is a single student, then three binary variables (*accounting*, *economics*, and *marketing*) could be generated. When either of the three binary variables take a value of 1, it indicates that the student is majoring in the respective field. A 0, on the other hand, indicates that the student is not majoring in that field.

To illustrate the use of categorical data, consider the dataset in Table 1.1. The dataset includes the characteristics of students taking an undergraduate course in business statistics. The first two columns of data – *Student* and *Dorm* – are

---

3 https://www.tdcj.state.tx.us/death_row/dr_executed_offenders.html
4 https://www.statcrunch.com/app/index.php?dataid=1004405
5 http://toddwschneider.com/posts/the-simpsons-by-the-data/
6 An ambitious chap shared a dataset classifying every bowel movement he made over 2 years. There is even a histogram. http://imgur.com/a/n5Gm0

Table 1.1 Student characteristics from an undergraduate course in business statistics.

Student	Dorm	Floor	GPA	SAT rank
Barry	Hawthorne	5	3.98	1
Cindy	Whittier	3	2.87	10
Stan	Dickinson	1	1.98	9
Donna	Dickinson	−1	4.00	2
Drew	Whittier	−2	3.20	5
Wilbur	Fairchild	0	2.56	6
Frank	Hawthorne	4	2.98	8
Jose	Emerson	2	3.12	7
Paul	Hawthorne	1	3.45	4
Steve	Emerson	5	3.88	3

categorical. This includes the student's first name and the name of the dorm each student lives in on campus. While it may be possible to apply codes to these categorical variables (e.g., student ID's in place of names) those numbers would just be used as an alternative way to categorize data and would not reflect magnitudes or ranking.

The remaining three variables: *Floor, GPA,* and *SAT Rank* in Table 1.1 are numeric. The variable *Floor* denotes which floor they live on in their respective dorm. The numbers follow European conventions with 0 being the ground floor and negative numbers indicating floors below ground. The variable *GPA* is the student's grade point average capped at 4.0, and the variable *SAT Rank* ranks each student in terms of their SAT score with 1 being the student with the highest SAT score.

1.2 Numerical Data

Numerical, or quantitative, data result from some form of counting, measurement or computation. Numeric data are broken down into variables that are *discrete* or *continuous*. Discrete data are typically thought of as variables that are *countable*, in which fractions do not make sense. Often, these are integer values, and examples include the number of courses taken, number of credit hours earned, number of children, number of flights, and the number of absences. You may notice that the terminology "number of" often precedes the description of a discrete variable. In our dataset in Table 1.1, the variables *Floor* and *SAT Rank* are both discrete numeric variables. Clearly, the number of floors is countable and fractions of a floor do not make sense.[7] The variable *SAT Rank* is also discrete. The SAT rankings are integer values, can be counted, and are definitely not divisible.

In contrast, continuous variables can take on any value within an interval. Continuous data are not counted, and is usually measured. With continuous data "fractions make sense." Examples include weight, speed, height, distance, prices, and interest rates. Even if continuous data are rounded so that only integer values are reported, the data are still continuous. Age, for example, is typically reported in integer values. However, age can be measured very precisely by years, days, minutes, seconds, milliseconds, and so on. The same is usually standard with prices and other financial data. These are continuous measures that are rounded for convenience. They are not counted. The variable *GPA* in Table 1.1 is continuous.

In the later chapters, we sometimes blur the lines between discrete and continuous data. For example, the number of votes candidates receive in a presidential election is discrete. Why? Because votes are counted and fractions do not make sense. However, when the range of values is so large (e.g., millions of votes) that the difference between one unit (e.g., one vote) is so small, we sometimes treat discrete data to be continuous.

1.3 Level of Measurement

When data are categorical (or qualitative), the level of measurement is called *nomimal*. Nominal data have no meaningful order and any numbers attributed to data values are simply for coding purposes. Denoting female observations with the number 1 and male observations with the number zero is an example. The numbers are not meaningful on their own and the numbers could be substituted with any other numbers without affecting the results. Dividing your classmates into geeks, dweebs, and nerds, for instance, would require nominal measurement. Simply coding students in one category, even if it is numeric, has no meaning in terms of relative rank. The level of measurement for the two categorical variables *Student* and *Dorm* in Table 1.1 is nominal.

Data that are *ordinal* in nature suggest that there is a meaningful ranking among the data, but there is no clear measurement regarding the distances between values. Placement in a race for instance could be denoted as first, second, third, and so on. Without additional clarifying data, the rankings are meaningful because we know that the second place runner finished before the third place runner, but we do not know how much faster the second place runner was relative to the third place runner. Another example is placement in an

---

7 One exception is in the film "Being John Malkovich" in which many scenes took place on the 7.5 floor of the Mertin-Flemmer building.

Olympic event, where gold is better than silver that is better than bronze. However, those rankings do not convey how much better the gold medal winner was compared to the silver medal winner. Data on vehicle size could also be ordinal if it were classified as 3 = full size, 2 = compact, or 1 = subcompact. Clearly, 3 > 2 > 1 in terms of size, but it is unclear how much bigger a full-size car is compared to a subcompact car. In Table 1.1, the variable *SAT Rank* is ordinal. The ranking indicates which student scored higher in the SAT exam (one indicating the highest grade), but it does not tell us how far the first highest score is from the second, and so on.

Interval data are numeric and have both a meaningful ranking and measurable distances between values. The defining feature of interval data is that there is no *true* zero. With interval data, a zero does not mean that the variable has no value. Temperature is the classic example. A temperature of zero degree Celsius does not mean there is an absence of temperature. Without a true zero, the numeric values cannot be divided or multiplied and still retain their meaning. A temperature of 20 degrees, for example, is not twice as warm as 10 degrees. The intervals between measures can be interpreted with precision (e.g., there is a 10-degree difference between 10 and 20 degrees), but we cannot say that 20 degrees is twice as warm. However, it is still possible to calculate an average with interval data (e.g., average temperature) and measures of variability. The variable *Floor* in Table 1.1 is interval data. A zero value does not mean the absence of a floor, it is simply a reference point. This reference point can change, for example in the United States, the ground floor of most buildings is typically a positive number. Interval data may be discrete or continuous.

The final category of measurement is *ratio*. Ratio data are like interval data except that there is a true zero. Examples include weight, height, speed, the number of children, number of classes, number of votes, calories, and grades. GPA is ratio data. Even though we do not observe a zero value for GPA, a value of zero is still meaningful. Ratio data may be discrete or continuous.

1.4 Cross-Sectional, Time-Series, and Panel Data

Another way to characterize data is by time period. When a dataset consists of observations from different individual units (e.g., people, businesses, and countries) in the same time period, we call that *cross-sectional data*. You can think of cross-sectional data as information taken from one single slice in time. US census data are cross-sectional since it consists of all individual households in a given year. The data in Table 1.1 are cross-sectional, because they consist of characteristics of 10 students in the same undergraduate business statistics course.

Time-series data, on the other hand, track observations over time. Often, time-series data follow one single individual unit (e.g., person, business, and country) over a time period. For example, tracking the daily Dow Jones industrial average over a period of 10 years would constitute a time-series dataset. Each observation is a different point in time (e.g., day, month, year, and decade). Another example is a dataset tracking temporal changes in a single company's stock price. Climate scientists rely on time-series data to understand trends in the average temperature of the earth and how those measurements interact with carbon emissions.

It is often useful to plot time-series data using a *line chart* to get a feel for specific trends, cycles, or seasons. To illustrate, consider the dataset in Table 1.2. The dataset includes voting results for every American presidential election after World War II. The data include the year, the candidate's name by party, total votes for both the democratic and republican candidates, and aggregate votes. The dataset in Table 1.2 can be considered to be time-series data. Each observation is from a different year, and the individual units are unique pairs of democratic and republican presidential candidates.

The data from Table 1.2 are plotted as a line chart in Figure 1.1. The Figure shows an increasing trend in the number of votes for candidates from both

Table 1.2 American presidential election voting results (in millions) post World War II.

Year	Democrat	Republican	Dem vote	Rep vote	Total vote
1948	Truman	Dewey	24.11	21.97	46.07
1952	Stevenson	Eisenhower	27.31	33.78	61.09
1956	Stevenson	Eisenhower	26.74	35.58	62.32
1960	Kennedy	Nixon	34.23	34.11	68.33
1964	Johnson	Goldwater	42.83	27.15	69.97
1968	Humphrey	Nixon	30.99	31.71	62.70
1972	McGovern	Nixon	28.90	46.74	75.64
1976	Carter	Ford	40.83	39.15	79.97
1980	Carter	Reagan	35.48	43.64	79.12
1984	Mondale	Reagan	37.45	54.17	91.62
1988	Dukakis	Bush Sr.	41.72	48.64	90.36
1992	Bill Clinton	Bush Sr.	44.86	38.80	83.66
1996	Bill Clinton	Dole	47.40	39.20	86.60
2000	Gore	Bush Jr.	51.00	50.47	101.46
2004	Kerry	Bush Jr.	58.89	61.87	120.77
2008	Obama	McCain	69.46	59.93	129.39
2012	Obama	Romney	65.92	60.93	126.85
2016	Hillary Clinton	Trump	65.85	62.99	128.84

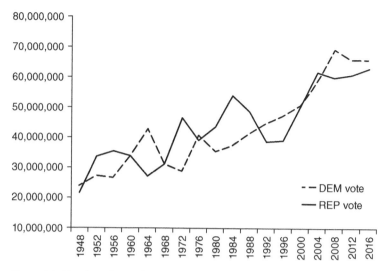

Figure 1.1 Number of votes for each party in U.S. presidential elections after World War II.

parties over time. Since the population is growing, it is unsurprising to see an increase in the total number of votes. What is more interesting is how the Figure shows repeated cycles in which one party votes more than the other.

When a dataset has multiple individual units and observations are taken at different points of time, we call that *panel data*. Tracking the stock price for multiple companies over a 5-year period would be panel data. Another example would be data on the number of regular season wins over a span of 15 years for all 30 teams in Major League Baseball.

1.5 Summary

The starting point with a course in statistics is understanding the differences in the types of data you may encounter. Data are categorical (qualitative) or numerical (quantitative). Categorical data are described by words rather than numbers. Measurement for these variables is classified as *nominal*, and they cannot be ordered in any meaningful way. Numeric data can be either discrete (countable – fractions do not make sense) or continuous (uncountable – fractions make sense). Measurement for numeric data can be *ordinal* – can be ordered, but there is no measurable distance between values, *interval* – can be ordered, distances between values can be measured, but there is no true zero, or *ratio* – like interval data, but there is a true zero. Finally, data taken from one point in time is cross-sectional, and data tracking values over a time period is time series. When a dataset includes both cross-sectional and time series, we call that a panel dataset.

2

Populations and Samples

The summer of 2015 was a particularly menacing one for shark attacks on the coast of North Carolina. There were a reported 33 shark attacks in a 6-week span in a state that had seen a total of 25 attacks in the past 10 years. Living in North Carolina at the time, these stories were big news. The incidents received a lot of national attention too. In response to the panic during the height of the attacks, the Washington Post published a story online that attempted to put the recent high frequency of reported shark attacks into perspective.[1] To do so, the story reported on the average number of deaths each year in the United States from animal encounters. They found, on average, that sharks kill one person per year. Other creatures that were considered included snakes, spiders, bees, cows, dogs, bears, and alligators. Dogs, for instance, kill 28 people in an average year. Part of the take-away message was that shark attacks and fatalities are very rare indeed, even compared to other animal-related deaths. Continuing with the dog comparison, the article concluded that people are 28 times more likely to die from being attacked by a dog than being mauled by a shark.

If I can convince you of one thing in this chapter it is that the comparisons made in the Washington Post article are not very useful ones. The reason is that when comparing dog and shark fatalities simply by comparing their frequencies, the study implicitly defines the same *population* of interest for all animal attacks. To illustrate, suppose that the implicit population of interest is 320 million Americans (so every documented resident more or less). Using relative frequencies and the logic of the article, the likelihood of getting killed by a shark is 1/320,000,000 compared to the 28/320,000,000 likelihood of being killed by a dog. Since both metrics use the same denominator, it is clear that dog-related deaths are 28 times more frequent. The problem with this analysis is that the likelihood of getting killed by a shark or a dog is only positive if a person puts himself into a situation in which an encounter is possible. Most people probably do encounter dogs in their day-to-day life, and so maybe the

---

1 http://www.washingtonpost.com/news/wonkblog/wp/2015/06/16/chart-the-animals-that-are-most-likely-to-kill-you-this-summer/

entire population of Americans is the relevant population. However, a person can die from a shark attack only if he goes to a beach by an ocean that is populated with sharks and actually goes swimming. While I do not know how many Americans fit that description, I am certain, it is only a small segment of the total 320 million Americans. The point is that the likelihood of getting killed by a shark is not 1/320,000,000. For my parents, who have not swam in the ocean in 15 years, the probability of dying from a shark attack is zero. They are not part of the population of interest. But, for those who do swim in the Atlantic coast during the warm weather months, the probability of getting mauled by a shark is certainly higher than 1/320,000,000. As an example, if about 75 million people visit beaches and swim in the ocean each year, then that likelihood is 1/75,000,0000, making the comparison between shark and dog fatalities much different. In this case, a person is only 6.5 times more likely to be killed by a dog than a shark. The point is that when making statistical comparisons, the population of interest matters a great deal.

2.1 What is the Population of Interest?

The later chapters of this book are on the topic of inferential statistics. Inferential statistics is all about using a sample of data to shed light on some aspect of a population that there is uncertainty about. Let us use national political elections as an example. During any election season, the public is exposed to what seems like a never-ending stream of inferential statistics. Daily reports of a candidate's current percentage of supporters make headline news. For citizens to understand what the polling results mean requires an understanding of what the population is, and the population of interest can change, even within the same presidential campaign. During the primaries, for example, polls are interested in finding out which candidate *likely* voters favor within each party. Therefore, the population of interest is likely voters in a political party (see Figure 2.1). For example, in mid-June of 2008, Barack Obama had an estimated 52% of the Democratic party vote (compared with Hillary Clinton's 41%). The statistic was taken from a sample of 1500 drawn from the population of likely Democratic party voters. However, after the primary elections were finished and the candidates from the two parties were chosen, then the relevant population for the national polling agencies changed. At that point, polls are focused on inferring which candidate has a larger percentage of supporters of *all* likely American voters.

Clearly defining the population of interest is the starting point for any statistical analysis. There is no formula for doing this correctly. Rather, it requires careful thought about the research question. Suppose I wanted to find out how prevalent alcohol abuse is with students in higher education. Without any other qualifiers, the implied population of interest is very broad. The population consists of all students, in any higher education institution, in any part of the world at any point in time. If my question is really about the

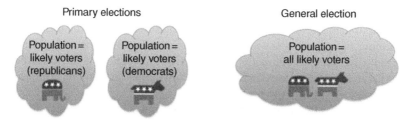

Figure 2.1 A comparison of populations of interest for political polls between the primary elections and the general election.

current levels of alcohol abuse in higher education in the United States, then the population of interest is different. The population in this case is all students currently enrolled in an American institution of higher education. The point is that in order to determine what the population of interest is, you first need a clearly focused question.

OK, suppose you have a clearly defined population you want to know something about. And further suppose that you cannot get your hands on data for the entire population. This could be for many reasons, but a lack of resources (e.g., time and money) is one of the most important ones. In order to learn something about the population in these cases, you need to take a *sample*. A sample is just a small subset, or fraction, of the population. Just a taste. That sample is going to give us an estimate (our best educated conjecture) about something we want to know. I know what you are asking yourself. How do we go about sampling from a population?

2.2 How to Sample From a Population?

A good sample is one that is a close representation of the larger population of interest. In other words, to the best of our abilities, we want to draw a sample that is not biased in any particular way relative to the population it is drawn from. Using the presidential primary election example from earlier, suppose we are interested in finding out how much support a certain Republican candidate has by conducting a survey. A good sample would be one that closely matches important characteristics of the larger voting population. Those characteristics, for example, may be age, gender, income, and geographic location (there could be many others as well). Achieving an unbiased, representative sample requires some degree of randomization. We will start with the simplest form.

2.2.1 Simple Random Sampling

In a *simple random sample*, every unit in the population has the same chance of being included in the sample. A good starting point is thinking about what types of processes would lead to random selections for a sample. Imagine you are a member of a statistics class of 50 students. Suppose the professor needs one student to help assist with passing out materials to the class. The professor has a number of options. She could, for example, call on the one nerd sitting in the front row (note: not all nerds sit in the front row, and not all front row students are nerds). That choice is not random, but simply convenient. Suppose as an alternative approach, the professor has an alphabetical list of students in descending order by last name and blindly picks one from the middle of the list. That choice is also not random because by restricting attention to the middle of the list, Johnny Appleseed and Frank Zappa have almost zero chance of being chosen while Phil Mickelson and Wolfgang Mozart have a decent shot. However, if the professor numbered each student from 1 to 50 (say in alphabetical order) and then rolled a 50-sided die (yes, they do exist), then that rolled number would be random and therefore the choice of student paired with that number would also be random. You could also use a simple computer program (e.g., using the formula = RANDBETWEEN(1,50) in Excel) to choose a random number between two bounds. Using a random number generator is therefore a process that can be utilized to create a random sample from a population.

To understand simple random sampling, it is sometimes helpful to work with an example in which the underlying population is known. Do not get confused here. In reality, we take a sample because we do not have access to the entire population, and therefore some aspects of the population are unknown. However, when learning about statistics, it is often useful to compare the results from sampling with known population values in order to shed light on how different sampling procedures can yield different results.

As an example, let us consider a population with historical relevance. Our population of interest is the collective of passengers aboard the *Titanic* in 1912. In total, 2224 passengers left Southampton, England, on the morning of April 15, 1912. Of course, only a fraction survived. Imagine we are interested in the percentage of passengers who survived the *Titanic* disaster. The population dataset is the entire passenger list and whether or not that passenger survived. Given this, we can consider how to draw a simple random sample of 100 passengers from the population of 2224 to estimate the percentage of passengers who survived. We will discuss how to determine appropriate sample sizes later in Chapter 7, but for now, we will consider a sample size of 100 passengers.

With simple random sampling, every passenger must have the same chance of being part of the sample. If all *Titanic* passengers were assigned a unique passenger number from 1 to 2224, and then a random number generator chose 100 unique numbers, then the passengers corresponding to those 100 numbers would make up our sample. When drawing multiple random numbers from a population, it is important to consider the implications of sampling with replacement and sampling without replacement. Using the RANDBETWEEN function in Excel to draw 100 numbers, for example, it is possible that the same number is repeated in the sample more than once. This is a type of sampling with replacement since any randomly chosen number is not removed from the population once it is drawn. Compare this to pulling an ID number randomly from a hat, and then not replacing that number. Continuing in this fashion for 100 draws would result in a sample taken without replacement. For our purposes, we are considering sampling 100 passengers from the population of *Titanic* passengers without replacement.

From the sample of 100, we would calculate the percentage of passengers who survived the crash. This sample value would be our estimate, which we call a *sample statistic*. Any value calculated from a sample is a sample statistic. Using Excel, I took a simple random sample of 100 and 35% of the passengers sampled survived. The sample is displayed in Figure 2.2. The population percentage of survivors, called the *population parameter*, is known to be 31.9% (711 of 2224). Note that the sample statistic is not equal to the population parameter, it is just an estimate. And if we had drawn a different sample of 100, we would likely get a different value, but it should be pretty close. Differences between sample statistics and population parameters are expected in sampling (this is called *sampling error*). Different samples may lead to different values for sample statistics, but the random nature of the methodology safeguards against potential biases.

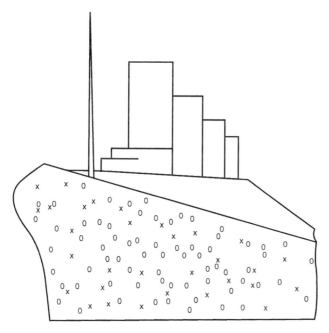

Figure 2.2 The figure illustrates a *simple random sample* of size 100 taken from the population of Titantic passengers. *x* indicates a survivor. In this example, 35 of the 100 passengers sampled survived the Titantic crash.

2.2.2 Stratified Sampling

Sometimes, it is possible to improve how representative a sample is by utilizing prior information about the population. Suppose the population can be broken down into subgroups such that each exhibits certain relevant characteristics. With the *Titanic*, it is likely that not all passengers had the same chance of survival when boarding the vessel. Women and children are typically given preference over adult males. Crew members commit to helping others before they help themselves. And, it might be the case that survival rates vary across passenger class. As depicted in Figure 2.3, we could divide the population of passengers into *strata*. Passengers are segmented by whether they are children, female, or male. In this example, we have three strata. Figure 2.3 also includes the percentage of the population (all passengers) who are part of each stratum.

Once you have the strata defined, the sampling method follows the same technique as simple random sampling except that samples are taken within each stratum. We would have three subsamples that would be combined to form our larger sample. The most important point is that the sample size from each stratum relative to the entire sample size is the same fraction as the population percentages. For example, since 5% of passengers are children, which means

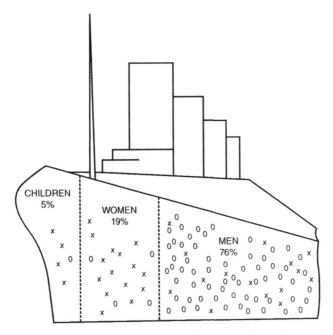

Figure 2.3 The figure illustrates a *stratified sample* of size 100 taken from the population of Titantic passengers. An *x* indicates a survivor. In this sample, 4 of 5 children survived, 15 of 19 women survived, and 14 of 76 men survived for a total of 33/100.

5% of the observations from our entire sample should come from this stratum. Given a total sample size of 100, it would mean that five observations should be drawn from the population of children. An example of a stratified random sample for the Titanic data is shown in Figure 2.3. When the data from each stratum are combined, our sample estimate of the survival rate of passengers is 33% (33 of the 100 sampled survived the crash). Compared with the simple random sample approach from above, the stratified sampling method leads to a closer estimate of the population survival rate. While this may not always be the case, stratified random sampling prevents the possibility of over or under-representing important subgroups.

Another approach to stratified sampling is to conduct a simple random sample and then weigh the data to reflect the percentages in each stratum. For instance, consider the sample size of 100 from the previous section on simple random sampling. Suppose that only 60% of the observations from that sample were from male passengers. Since the actual percentage of male passengers is 76%, the population percentage is 1.26 times larger than the sample percentage ($76/60 = 1.27$). In this case, those observations could be multiplied by a weight of 1.27 to match the population percentages. Other groups will be overrepresented and their weights would be less than one. This is considered a postsurvey method of stratified sampling.

2.2.3 Other Methods

While simple random and stratified sampling is the most common approach to data collection, there are other approaches worth mentioning. *Systematic sampling* is the approach of choosing every kth item from a sequence or a list. For example, given the *Titanic* passenger list, the sample could be compiled by choosing every fifth person on the list. Election day exit polling typically makes use of a mix of stratified and systematic sampling. The strata are voting districts, which are then randomly sampled. Then, pollsters use systematic sampling methods to compile the sample data from each randomly chosen voting site. For example, every 15th voter who exits the booth may be approached to see if they will complete a survey.[2] The method, like all sampling methods in practice, is not perfect. Not everyone who is approached agrees to participate. Therefore, even though every 15th voter may be approached, the gap between voters in the sample may be less precise. Not responding to an invitation to complete a survey triggers what is called *nonresponse bias*. The bias exists because those voters who are not willing to complete the survey are part of the population of interest, but by definition this group will be underrepresented in the sample. Nonresponse bias is a potential problem with any survey method.

---

2 see Levy, M. (1983) "The methodology and performance of election day polls." Public Opinion Quarterly 47:54–67.

Cluster sampling, another approach, is very similar to stratified sampling except that the strata are determined by geographic areas. For example, a state could be divided into counties and each county would be a stratum, and samples are drawn from each stratum. The percentage of the total sample taken from each county should mirror the percentage of the state's total population living in each county. Another technique that is commonly used, but not at all scientific is *convenience sampling*, which is a method of using a sample that is readily available or convenient. Common examples include web sites that invite their users to participate in online polls. Such samples are not random because people make a deliberate effort to access the site and only those who opt in to participate are part of the dataset. Another example of convenience sampling is a professor who uses student responses from their class to make broad inferences about students in general.

2.3   Getting the Data

A huge amount of sample data is gathered through surveys. Surveys are conducted over the phone (landline and/or cell phones), mail, personal interviews, and internet. Each survey method has its own advantages and limitations. A reputable research institution will try to blend different survey techniques with the goal of minimizing the types of bias each can contribute to the study. A web-based survey is going to preclude the subset of the population that does not go online, or that does not visit a particular web site or use a particular service. A survey posted on Facebook, for example, precludes sampling anyone who does not use Facebook. Only using landline telephones as a survey method would preclude many young people who only have cell phones, and only using cell phones would underrepresent the older population. Election polling, for example, typically relies on both landline and cell phone respondents, and uses in-person exit polls during election days.

Another common way data are gathered for analysis is through *experiments*. Clinical trials on new pharmaceuticals typically involve gathering multiple samples of participants, some of whom will be administered a new drug and others will be given a placebo. The results are usually measured (e.g., blood pressure) or gathered from direct observation (e.g., strength levels). The experimental method is also used in business and economics. Examples include using experiments to compare the effectiveness of different marketing strategies, sales techniques, economic and public policies, and compensation incentives.

In many cases, businesses and firms *self-report* data, in particular when required through government regulation. The United States Environmental Protection Agency, for example, requires regulated firms to report on their emissions levels of harmful pollutants. These reports include levels of pollutants such as sulfur dioxide and nitric oxide. In general, government agencies

Table 2.1 A list of useful data sources found online.

Bureau of Economic Analysis	www.bea.gov
Bureau of Labor Statistics	www.bls.gov
Central Intelligence Agency	www.cia.gov
Data.Gov	www.data.gov
Environmental Protection Agency	www.epa.gov
Federal Reserve System	www.federalreserve.gov
Food and Drug Administration	www.fda.gov
National Center for Education Statistics	www.nces.ed.gov
National Center for Health Statistics	www.cdc.gov/nchs
United States Census Bureau	www.census.gov
United States Federal Statistics	www.fedstats.gov
World Bank	www.worldbank.org
Word Health Organization	www.who.int/en

are often a good source of data, especially for undergraduate research projects. Of particular note, the web site www.data.gov hosts a collection of roughly 200,000 datasets that are publicly available and searchable by topic. We end this section with a list of other helpful data sources easily found on the web (Table 2.1).

2.4 Summary

All data-driven analysis requires a clear definition of the target population. Sometimes, it is possible to get information on an entire population (we call this a census). For example, suppose I was interested in determining the average GPA of the current students at a specific university in the United States. In this case, my population of interest is the entire student body at the university and it is likely that the registrar office has a record of each student's GPA. As a broader example, the United States Census Bureau attempts to compile a population dataset on key demographic variables every 10 years for people living in the United States. The method of assembling a population dataset varies depending on the nature of the variables of interest. A population dataset can be obtained through survey methods (e.g., US Census), record keeping (e.g., birth records, university records), or observation (e.g., number of polar bears in existence). However, for many research questions, the population dataset is not available. This can be for many reasons. Sometimes, a population is finite (e.g., current US citizens), but in other cases, the population of interest is effectively infinite. If, for example, you are interested in determining whether children are better behaved after they have been punished in response to bad behavior, then the population of interest is children, which is constantly changing. In this case, a population dataset is not available. In other cases, the population data exist but it is not feasible, or too expensive and time consuming to obtain. In these cases, population values must be *estimated* using sample data. In this chapter, we explored established methods used to draw representative samples from a given population.

3

Descriptive Statistics

During my second semester teaching undergraduate statistics, I started one of the classes by presenting the following quote: "the average person has one breast and one testicle." I did not discuss the statistic, it was simply displayed on the screen while I prepared materials for the class. When this particular class finished, a slightly timid male student came to the front of the room to talk with me. The class had over 90 students in it, so he first introduced himself. And then, he told me how shocked he was to learn that the average person has only one testicle, and before I could reply he shared that he had one of his testicles removed when he was younger. He finished with "I didn't know it was that common." I paused for a second to figure out how to break the news to him gently. I told him that while the statistic seems to be odd at first, since the gender divide between humans is roughly 50–50, it is a sensible rough estimate. Most men do have two testicles, and since most women have zero, on average people have one. I told him that I introduce this statistic because it gets students thinking about what the average tells us and how in some circumstances the average can be tremendously misleading. From the color of his face, I knew he understood. He and I would later joke about it throughout the semester.

The average, or mean, is what we call a descriptive statistic. Descriptive statistics are the topic for this chapter. In Chapter 2, we focused on defining the population of interest and how to draw random samples from that population. In this chapter, we start "looking" at the data (both populations and samples). In general, there are two ways to look at, or describe, data: visually and numerically. Most primary textbooks in business statistics dedicate a chapter to describing data visually. The material usually includes instructions on how to create and interpret pie charts, histograms, line graphs, box and whisker plots, scatter plots, and many others. While each of these methods for illustrating data can be useful, when they are lumped together without context, their importance tends to get lost on students. From experience, the chapter on describing data visually is somewhat tedious, blasting figures and graphs one after another with very little practical motivation. In this text, we will deal with visual descriptions

A Guide to Business Statistics, First Edition. David M. McEvoy.
© 2018 John Wiley & Sons, Inc. Published 2018 by John Wiley & Sons, Inc.

of data, but they will be peppered throughout the book in the context and situations in which they are needed.

A set of data, whether it is from a population or a sample, is typically described by three characteristics. First, we want to know something about where the data are *centered* or concentrated. Second, we want to know how much *variability* there is in the data, and third we want to get a feel for the general *shape* of the data. We will discuss each of these characteristics in this chapter. We begin with a population dataset that we can use to illustrate the concepts. For our example, we turn to the subject of violent crime in the United States. Crime statistics are some of the most used and abused statistics in public policy debates. At a single point in time, a state could be considered both very safe and very dangerous depending on how crime is measured. Take Alaska for instance. Every year Alaska has a low frequency of violent crimes compared to the other 49 states. By the naïve measure of the total crimes, it is a relatively safe state. However, when crimes are measured per capita, it is the most dangerous state in the United States (only D.C. is more dangerous). Both measures – the total crimes and per-capita crimes – are based on facts. To be active and informed citizens, we need to understand a bit about statistics, how they are calculated, what they tell us, and, most importantly, what the limitations are.

The violent crime rate for every state and Washington, D.C., in 2014 is contained in Table 3.1. The crime rate is calculated as the number of violent crimes per 100,000 people.[1]

3.1 Measures of Central Tendency

A good starting point for describing data is identifying a central position, which is either where data values are concentrated or a value that is in the middle of the dataset. Since a central position can mean different things, we have different measures of central tendency (but we have our favorites). We start with the most frequently used and therefore the most important measure, the mean.

3.1.1 The Mean

In statistics, we can use the terms *mean* and *average* interchangeably. Statisticians love to have different names for the same thing, so you will have to get used to it. In any event, the *mean* or average is calculated by adding up all the values and dividing by the total number of values. Using our dataset, the mean of the population is 364.41 violent crimes per 100,000 people (see Formula A.1). Whenever we calculate something from population data,

---

1 Source: The US Federal Bureau of Investigation's Uniform Crime Reporting (UCR) program.

Table 3.1 Violent crime rates in the United States in 2014 (per 100,000 people).

D.C.	1244	California	396	Mississippi	279
Alaska	636	Massachusetts	391	Iowa	274
Nevada	636	New York	382	North Dakota	265
Tennessee	608	Georgia	377	New Jersey	261
New Mexico	597	Illinois	370	Hawaii	259
Florida	541	Indiana	365	Connecticut	237
Louisiana	515	Kansas	349	Oregon	232
South Carolina	498	North Carolina	330	Minnesota	229
Delaware	489	South Dakota	327	Rhode Island	219
Arkansas	480	Montana	324	Utah	216
Maryland	446	Pennsylvania	314	Idaho	212
Missouri	443	Colorado	309	Kentucky	212
Alabama	427	West Virginia	302	Virginia	196
Michigan	427	Wisconsin	290	New Hampshire	196
Oklahoma	406	Washington	285	Wyoming	196
Texas	406	Ohio	285	Maine	128
Arizona	400	Nebraska	280	Vermont	99

we call that value a population parameter. Parameters are typically denoted with Greek letters, and we use the letter μ (pronounced "mew") to denote the population mean. So, for the 2014 violent crime rates in the United States, $\mu = 364.41$. From the values in Table 3.1, we see that Indiana is the closest to being the "average" state with a violent crime rate of 365. It turns out that Indiana is known for being average, not just in crime. Business Insider published a study that ranked states from "weirdest" to "most normal."[2] Number one? Indiana.

The mean is a useful measure of central tendency for a couple of reasons. (1) The mean uses all of the data, so we are not missing any information with this measure. (2) The mean is a perfect balance of the data in the sense that positive and negative deviations from the mean exactly offset each other. For example, Vermont – arguably the safest state – witnessed 99 violent crimes per 100,000, which is 265.41 less than the average. This a negative deviation from the mean. Meanwhile, Alaska had 636 crimes per 100,000 people, which is 271.59 crimes greater than the mean (a positive deviation). If we add up all the deviations, both positive and negative, from the population of 50 states and D.C. it would sum to zero.

---

2 http://www.businessinsider.com/state-normalness-ranking-2015-10/

The weakness of using the mean as a measure of central location is that it is affected by extreme values. The number of violent crimes in Washington D.C. is over 600 more than the next highest state. This high crime rate pulls the average up by quite a bit. Indeed, if we calculated the average salary without D.C., we get 346.82, which tells us that D.C.'s crime rate alone pulls the mean up by just over 17.

Because the mean is very sensitive to extreme values, it is less useful as a measure of central tendency for some common metrics. In general, data on salaries and income are often significantly affected by a small number of high earners. The average salary of Americans is much higher than what most Americans earn and this is because the 1% of people at the top income bracket pull that average up substantially. The visual I have is Bill Gates and Warren Buffet yanking on a pulley to lift the average up. The introductory example of the average person having "one breast and one testicle" is another reason to sometimes be cautious of the mean. The mean can be misleading. For example, a city that experiences extreme high temperatures and extreme lows may have a very pleasant average temperature even though that average temperature may never be realized. In this case, the "average" temperature has nothing to do with the "typical" temperature. As another example, the Millennium Force roller coaster in Cedar Point, Ohio, is one of the tallest and fastest in the world. It is an absolute beast. Riders experience a drop of 300 feet at 80 degrees reaching a speed of 93 miles/hour. However, it has an average speed of roughly 22 miles/hour, which is safe for most children and elderly. Your Great Aunt Mary might be in for quite a surprise if she puts too much stock in the average speed when deciding whether to brave the Millennium Force.

Of course, in many circumstances, you will be working with a sample of data drawn from a larger population, and we can also calculate the mean for a sample of data. Let us look at an example in which we have a sample of data. For some of my academic research projects, I use the online workplace Amazon Mechanical Turk (called *MTurk*) to generate data. MTurk has thousands of workers who get paid to complete various tasks, from answering surveys to editing screen plays. As part of designing a research survey, I needed an estimate of how long it would take respondents to read a particular passage. Of course, I did not have population data on how long it would take *all* potential respondents to read the passage. So, I gathered a small sample of 30 people and kept track of how long it took each of them to read the passage (and answer a comprehension question). This sample is in Table 3.2.

The *sample mean* is calculated by adding up the times for the 30 respondents and then dividing by 30, which is 2.97 minutes. The formula for the population mean and the sample mean is the same, however the notation is different. The sample mean is denoted as $\bar{x}$ (called x bar), and here $\bar{x} = 2.97$. The sample mean is the best estimate we have of a population mean when the parameter value

Table 3.2 Minutes required to read a short passage.

2.22	4.33
2.32	4.24
3.25	4.35
4.11	1.38
1.97	2.81
1.65	4.55
0.97	1.28
2.43	1.72
4.58	2.33
3.50	2.47
2.38	4.39
3.49	3.40
2.25	3.75
3.33	2.99
3.35	3.19

is unknown. Using this sample mean, I estimated that the average respondent would take about 3 minutes to read the passage.

3.1.2 The Median

Another measure of central tendency, and one that is particularly useful for data on income or wealth measures is the median. The *median* is the value in the middle of the dataset. The median is the 50th *percentile* – the value for which 50% of observations are smaller and 50% of observations are larger. The median is located by sorting your data from the smallest to largest and finding the value that splits the number of observations into two equal halves. If you have an odd number of observations, then it must be the case that one single value lies directly in the middle of your sorted data. For example, if you have nine observations ranked the smallest to largest, the fifth observation is the middle, or median value. For any dataset, you can locate the median value by first dividing the total number of observations by two. If the solution is not an integer (meaning, your answer is a fraction), then you simply round up to the next integer value to locate the median. If, for example, there were 89 observations, the location of the median value is 45 (because $89/2 = 44.5$). Alternatively, if the solution to dividing the total number of observations by two results in an integer, then there is no single value that equally divides the dataset in two. In this case, the median will be the *average* of the two numbers that can divide the dataset into two. Suppose we had a dataset of 100 observations. Since $100/2 =$ 50, the median value is going to be the average of the 50th and 51st value in the dataset.

The median crime rate from our population dataset of violent crime rates for the 50 states plus D.C. is from South Dakota. Dividing 51 by two yields 25.5, so the median crime rate is the 26th highest crime rate which is South Dakota's rate of 327.

3.1.3   The Mode

The *mode* is the most frequent value in a dataset. In Table 3.1, the mode, or modal value, is 196 crimes. Three states, Virginia, New Hampshire, and Wyoming witnessed a crime rate of 196. The usefulness of the mode, however, is very limited. In some cases, there is no mode, or there are multiple modes in the sense that a few values repeatedly appear but not one more than another. Moreover, sometimes the value that appears the most is not a value that is a good indication of central position. For our dataset, 196 is on the lower end of the distribution of crime rates for 2014. While it is the value that occurs most frequently, it is not indicative of the crime rate for the majority of the country. In other words, while 196 is the modal crime rate, it does not provide useful information about what the center of the dataset looks like.

3.2   Measures of Variability

The second way we describe data is by how variable it is. The mean and/or median can provide a feel for where the data are centered, but we often want to know whether most of the data hover around those figures or are they really spread out. We have some simple measures for variability. One measure is the *range* which is simply the largest value minus the smallest value. When reporting on grades in my statistics classes, I have noticed that students are always curious about the range. Did someone earn 100? Did someone totally bomb it? The range, however, is very limited in its usefulness. It is based on only the two most extreme values. With just the range as a measure we are left wondering about the variability of the rest of the data. What's going on with the data within the range? And since I know you too have these burning questions, I do not want to leave you hanging. Here, we present the two most useful measures of variability, the variance and standard deviation. As we move toward inferential statistics (hypotheses testing and regression), these measures become very important.

3.2.1   Variance and Standard Deviation

The *variance* is a measure of variation that uses every value in the dataset. The goal of the variance is to find out, on average, how much the values in our dataset differ from the mean. However, we cannot simply add up all the deviations from the mean and then divide by the number of data points. This is because, for values greater than the mean, the deviations are positive and for values less than the mean the deviations are negative and when you add them together you get zero. That leaves us with a couple of options. We could either take the absolute value of the deviations or we could square the deviations. The average of the absolute value of the deviations is called the *mean absolute deviation* (see Formula A.3).

Our chosen measure of variability – the variance – requires squaring the deviations from the mean. Once each deviation between a value and the mean is squared, we sum all of those squared values. When calculating a variance for a population dataset (i.e., the *population variance*), we then divide the sum of the squared deviations by the number of observations. The population variance therefore is an average of the squared deviations from the mean. The notation for the population variance is the lower case Greek letter sigma squared; that is, σ^2. The odd part about the variance is that the units are now squared. For example, the variance for the 2014 violent crime data is in crimes squared per 100,000 people. To better communicate this measure of variability, we want to get it back to the original units. We do this by taking the square root of the variance, which yields the *population standard deviation*, which gets rid of the squared term. Using Formula A.5, we find that the standard deviation for our population of state-level crime rates is $\sigma = 177.25$ crimes. Loosely speaking, we can interpret this finding by saying that the average deviation from the mean crime rate is 177.25.

Because the variance and standard deviation are calculated relative to the mean, they too are sensitive to extreme values. For example, if we excluded Washington D.C. – the most extreme value in the crime dataset – the standard deviation drops from 177.25 to 127.53, roughly 50 crimes. Extreme values, in either direction, increase the standard deviation of a dataset.

The variation in sample datasets (as opposed to population datasets) is also described by its variance and standard deviation. The sample variance and standard deviation, however, are sample statistics not population parameters (so we do not use Greek letters). The *sample variance* is denoted as s^2 and the *sample standard deviation* is denoted as s. These sample statistics are the best estimates we have of the population variance and standard deviation when these values are unknown. Although the interpretation of the standard deviation (again loosely: the average deviation from the mean) is the same for both populations or samples, the formulas do differ slightly. While the population variance is calculated by dividing by the total number of observations, the sample variance is calculated by dividing by the total number of observations minus 1 (see Formula A.6). The expression of (sample size − 1) is called the *degrees of freedom*. In general, the degrees of freedom for a statistic are equal to the number of values minus the number of statistics that were calculated on route to the one you are after. In order to estimate the variance using our sample, we first need to calculate the sample mean $\bar{x}$, so we subtract one. Degrees of freedom will show up as part of many formulas in a business statistics course (the formula for degrees of freedom will take different forms), and when you see this term, it means that you are calculating a statistic for which at least one other statistic is required as part of the process. The sample standard deviation is simply the square root of the sample variance (see Formula A.7).

For the sample dataset in Table 3.2 on how many minutes it took 30 respondents to read a passage online, the sample standard deviation is $s = 1.05$ minutes. Therefore, the average deviation from mean reading time is about 1 minute.

3.3 The Shape

The third way we describe data is by its shape. At first, it may seem odd to think about the "shape" of a dataset. Is not a dataset just a bunch of numbers? Well, what we mean by shape is the form the data take on when they are organized in a certain way. The starting point is organizing the data from the smallest to the largest. The next step is constructing a *histogram* of the dataset. This is achieved by splitting the entire range of the dataset into segments, often called "bins." The bins are just smaller ranges within the overarching data range. For example, a dataset of exam grades may go from 0 (Johnny Slackerstein) to 100 (Sally Studyhard – she kept her maiden name) and can be segmented into bins of roughly size 10. We could form bins from 0 to 10, another from 10.01 to 20, 20.01 to 30, and so on. This is really up to you. The number of bins to include is subjective, but a guiding rule is that you want enough segments to capture the variation of the data, but without having so many or so few that it makes it hard to discern a shape.

The histogram in Figure 3.1 illustrates the shape of the violent crime rate data in the United States. Each bin covers a range of 200 crimes, from 0 to over 1200. The bars show the number of states in each bin (labeled "frequency" on the vertical axis). Most states witnessed between 200 and 400 violent crimes in 2014 (34 of 51 fall into this bin), and all but one observation is between 99 and 636. The high crime rate in D.C. pulls the tail to the right.

A dataset that is symmetric is one in which the left side of the mean is the mirror image of the right side of the mean. One easy way to tell whether a dataset is symmetric or whether it is skewed is by comparing the median and the mean from the same dataset. If the mean = median, then the data are *symmetric*. Whenever the mean is different than the median, it indicates that the distribution of data is skewed in one direction. When the mean is larger than the median, the dataset is skewed to the right (or *right-skewed*). In our example, the mean crime rate for the United States is higher than the median crime

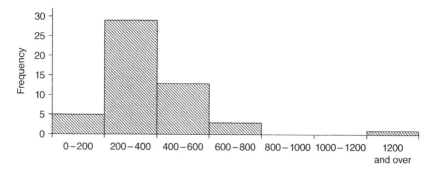

Figure 3.1 Crime rates in the United States in 2014.

rate (364.41 vs. 327), and therefore we know that the dataset is right-skewed. Right-skewed distributions are also common with data on income and wealth. Income data are right-skewed because a small number of people tend to earn large amounts of money. Visually, a dataset is skewed in the direction of its tail.

As another example, I will use data from the first exam from my business statistics course in the spring of 2016. There were 92 students in the class. The mean for exam 1 was 76 and the median was 80.[3] Right away, we know that since the median is greater than the mean, the dataset is *left-skewed*. This is of course typical with grade distributions. This is because a handful of people typically score very low grades whereas most people are in the 60–100 range. Those few slackers bring down the mean quite a bit but have a small impact on the median. You slackers know who you are.

Figure 3.2 contains a histogram that illustrates the shape of the distribution of exam grades. Each bar contains the frequency (i.e., the number) of grades in

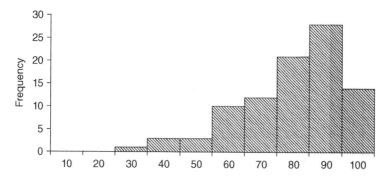

Figure 3.2 Exam grades from a business statistics course with 92 students.

---

3 The modal grade was an 84, the highest grade was 100, and the lowest was a 24 (range = 76). Finally, the standard deviation of the data was roughly 15.

that particular range. The bin labeled 10 contains the number of grades from 0 to 10 (there were zero of those). Likewise, the bin labeled 50 indicates the number of students scoring between 40 and 50 (three unhappy students found themselves in this bin).

Knowing the shape of a dataset can be important when trying to understand how things vary in a population or a sample. Consider the example of exam grades. The standard deviation of the grade data is 15 (points). From the histogram, it is clear that most of the data is within two standard deviations relative to the mean. Two standard deviations below the mean is $76 - 30 = 46$ and two standard deviations above is $76 + 30 = 106$. In fact, only four students scored out of that range (4.3%). In other words, about 95% of the data is within two standard deviations of the mean. It turns out that we have a formula that can estimate what percentage of all data in a distribution can be found within a certain number of standard deviations around the mean. The formula actually produces a conservative estimate – meaning in reality, the range is probably tighter – and it can be used for any distribution of data that take on any shape. The formula is attributed to Pafnuty *Chebyshev*, a Russian mathematician from the nineteenth century. You will never forget that name. Say it out loud. Chebyshev. It just rolls off the tongue. Cheby's theorem (or formula) is quite easy to use. Suppose you want to estimate what percentage of any dataset is within two standard deviations from the mean. Denote the number of standard deviations from the mean with the letter k, so here $k = 2$. Then, just calculate $1 - 1/k^2$, which yields 0.75. So by Chebyshev's theorem, we can be confident that *at least* 75% of any dataset lies within two standard deviations on the either side of the mean.

While Chebyshev's theorem is useful, we can be much more precise in describing data if we know more about the specific shape of the dataset we are working with. There are many distributions to learn in statistics, but by far the most important for a course in business statistics is the normal distribution. Chapter 5 is dedicated entirely to the normal distribution and how normally distributed data can be described. Before we get there, however, we will take a short departure into the world of probability in Chapter 4. We need to understand probability before diving deep into the normal distribution.

3.4 Summary

The goal of this chapter was to introduce the three ways we describe distributions of data: where is it *centered*, how does it *vary*, and what is the *shape*? While many measures exist, we concentrated in particular on the mean for our measure of central tendency and the variance/standard deviation for the measure of variability. These metrics will be used repeatedly throughout this text and they take important roles once we enter into inferential statistics. Recall that descriptive statistics is the topic of describing data that we have from either a population or a sample (the topic of this chapter) and inferential statistics uses sample data to infer or estimate something we do not know about a population of data (coming up). Learning how to describe data is a necessary starting point before introducing how to use data for inference. Last but not least, we also learned a bit about crime rates in the United States and just how "average" the state of Indiana really is.

Technical Appendix

The *population mean* is denoted by the Greek letter μ. The summation symbol Σ tells us to add up all the x_i values where the subscript i indexes observations from 1 to N.

$$\mu = \frac{\sum_{i=1}^{N} x_i}{N}.$$ (A.1)

The *sample mean* is denoted as $\bar{x}$ and is calculated as:

$$\bar{x} = \frac{\sum_{i=1}^{n} x_i}{n},$$ (A.2)

where lower case n denotes the sample size. The *mean absolute deviation* of a population is

$$\text{MAD} = \frac{\sum_{i=1}^{n} |x_i - \mu|}{N}.$$ (A.3)

The *population variance* is denoted as σ^2 and is calculated as:

$$\sigma^2 = \frac{\sum_{i=1}^{N} (x_i - \mu)^2}{N}.$$ (A.4)

Note that the population variance is in units squared. To get back to the original units, we take the square root which leads to the *population standard deviation*:

$$\sqrt{\sigma^2} = \sigma.$$ (A.5)

The *sample variance* and *sample standard deviation* are calculated in a similar way. The differences in comparison to the calculations for the population parameters can be observed in the formula for the sample variance. The numerator has the sample mean $\bar{x}$ in place of the population mean. Because we had to first use the sample of data to calculate $\bar{x}$ on route to calculating the variance, we divide by the *degrees of freedom* which is the sample size n minus 1.

$$s^2 = \frac{\sum\limits_{i=1}^{n}(x_i - \bar{x})^2}{n-1}. \qquad (A.6)$$

We again take the square root of the sample variance to get to the sample standard deviation:

$$\sqrt{s^2} = s. \qquad (A.7)$$

4

Probability

We live in a world of uncertainty. You cannot even be certain you will finish this sentence. Or this one. OK, you made it, but you get the point. Most of the decisions we make in life are made under uncertainty, and most of the consequences of those decisions are uncertain as well. If you are reading this book as part of a course in statistics, then you are likely pursuing a degree in higher education. On the other hand, if you are reading this book simply out of enjoyment, then you are crazy. That is one thing we can be certain about. In the likely case that this book is being used toward a degree program, your choice of what degree to pursue is made under tremendous uncertainty. You cannot be sure what career options will be available when you graduate, how much you will earn, whether you will relocate, or whether you will want to.

In the midst of uncertainty, we often want to know the *likelihood*, or *chance*, of certain events happening. Before leaving the house, for example, we may check the weather on our phones or on a weather channel. In doing so, we are informed about the chance of specific events occurring – like rain or snow – presented in percentage terms. For example, the weather channel may report a 90% chance of rain today. We then use that information to make decisions about how to dress and what to bring to protect ourselves from the rain. When the chance is 10% we might leave behind the umbrella, but at 99% we will take it. Thinking again about your degree and potential career choice, it might be useful to determine how likely it is that you will find a job after graduation. The determinants of whether or not you get a job are many, and some of them will depend directly on your performance as a student, what college or university you graduate from and your personality. However, whether you get the job you want also depends on how many jobs will be available and how many graduates will be applying for those positions. If there are more jobs than qualified graduates, then your chances are probably high. If, for example, there are only jobs available for half of all graduates, then the odds of landing the job are going to be lower.

The *probability* is the chance, in numeric terms, of a specific event occurring. We will analyze probabilities in this chapter for two main reasons.

A Guide to Business Statistics, First Edition. David M. McEvoy.
© 2018 John Wiley & Sons, Inc. Published 2018 by John Wiley & Sons, Inc.

The first is that understanding probabilities in general is very helpful with decision-making, both personally and professionally. Indeed, in order to think critically about the information we encounter each day, we need to know something about probabilities. The second reason we study probabilities is because they play a very important role in topics in inferential statistics like confidence intervals, hypotheses testing, and regression. In my experience as a statistics instructor, many students struggle with the probabilities section of the course. There are a few reasons for this. Many of the probabilities we want to calculate are *conditional*, that is, they depend on the outcome of other events. For example, we could estimate the probability that you will live to be 85 years old. Alternatively, we could estimate the probability that you will live to 85 years old conditional on whether you are a smoker. Or, we could estimate the probability that you will live to 85 years old conditional on whether you are smoker and you are overweight. And so on. So, there are many things to keep track of that make these problems challenging. This leads to the other reason students struggle. The formulas for all the different types of probabilities are not very approachable. There are all kinds of mathematical symbols that distract from the nature of the problem. And there is a whole new vocabulary that is introduced that often gets in the way of students' understanding. The goal of this chapter is strip away some of the distracting elements and walk through the core of the most important aspects of probability. We will use examples throughout. As always, the formulas can be found in the Technical Appendix to this chapter.

4.1   Simple Probabilities

Simple or *classical* probabilities are those that can be determined simply because of the nature of the study taking place. A coin flip is a good example. There are two possible outcomes (outcomes are also often called *events* in statistics) when flipping a coin, either heads or tails. When a coin is considered "fair," it means that getting a heads or a tails is equally likely. So, the probability of getting one outcome, heads for example, is easy to compute. There are two possibilities that are equally likely, so the probability of getting a heads is $1/2 = 0.50$. Of course the probability of landing a tails is the same. Something important to note right away is that probabilities are computed as relative events. The probability of flipping a coin and landing a heads is computed by considering that particular outcome relative to all possible outcomes. For this reason, probabilities will always be between zero and one. If for some reason we were playing with a trick coin that had heads on both sides, then the probability of flipping a heads is computed as $1/1 = 1$ and the probability of getting a tails is $0/1 = 0$.

Consider flipping a single "fair" coin twice. The probability of getting a heads on the first flip is 0.5. What is the probability of getting a heads on the second flip? Because the two events (flipping coins) are *independent*, the probability of getting a heads on the second flip is also 0.5. If two events are independent, then the probability of one event occurring is not affected by the probability of the other event occurring. Getting a heads or a tails on the first flip of a coin does not influence the probability of getting a heads or a tails on the second flip. Let us compare this with another set of events that are not independent. Suppose, I had a box with ten marbles in it, five are red and five are black and I am going to blindly choose two marbles consecutively. For each draw, what is the probability of choosing a red marble if we do not replace the marbles? This is called sampling without replacement. The probability of choosing a red marble on the first draw is $5/10 = 0.5$, just like flipping a coin. However, the probability of choosing a red marble on the second draw, *given* that I already chose a red marble on the first is not 0.5. The two draws are *dependent* events because the probability of the second draw depends on the outcome of the first draw. After choosing a red marble with my first choice, there are now nine marbles left, and only four of them are red. So, the probability of choosing a red marble on my second draw is $4/9 = 0.44$. Combining the two, the probability of drawing two red marbles consecutively without replacement is $5/10 \times 4/9 = 0.22$. If we replaced the marbles after each draw (i.e., sampling with replacement), then the two draws are independent events. In this case, the probability of choosing a red marble is 0.5 both times.

Another example where simple probabilities come into play is rolling a six-sided die (Figure 4.1).

If a die is fair, then each of the six sides is equally likely to result from a single roll. The probability of any of the six outcomes is simply $1/6$. Another important point is that for a single roll, only one outcome is possible. So, if you roll a

Figure 4.1 All possible outcomes (events) from one roll of a six-sided die.

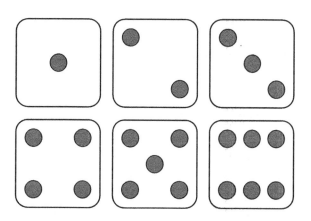

six that excludes the possibility of rolling anything else. We call these kinds of events *mutually exclusive*, meaning that when one outcome occurs (like rolling a six), the other outcomes cannot also occur. Heads and tails from a single coin flip are also mutually exclusive events. If all possible outcomes are mutually exclusive, then it must be the case that the probabilities of each outcome add up to one.

Now let us get crazy and roll two dice at the same time. (see statistics can be fun.) In this situation, we will observe a pair of numbers, one from each die. How many different pairs are possible? To help visualize the process, all of the possible outcomes are displayed in Table 4.1.

Looking at Table 4.1, it is easy to see that there are 36 possible outcomes from rolling two dice. The 36 possibilities are calculated from the product of 6 rows × 6 columns. The same logic can be used to figure out how many possible outcomes can occur when rolling three dice. The answer is $6 \times 6 \times 6 = 216$. And so on. To practice, use this line of thinking to determine how many possible outcomes can occur if you flipped five coins at the same time. Easy, $2 \times 2 \times 2 \times 2 \times 2$ or, to simplify the notation, we use $2^5 = 32$.

Consider again rolling two dice. Now, what is the probability of rolling a 7 when adding together the two dice? We know that probabilities are computed relative to all the possible outcomes. So, we know that the denominator will be 36. The numerator will be how many possible pairs add up to 7. First, think about the combinations that could add to 7. There are three: 3 and 4, 5 and 2, and 6 and 1. Each of these combinations can occur in two ways. For example, you could get 3 and 4 or 4 and 3. In total, there are six ways that we could roll a pair that add to 7. The probability of rolling a 7 with two dice therefore is $6/36 = 1/6$.

4.1.1 When to Add Probabilities Together

Paying so close attention to probabilities, it is no wonder that most statisticians shy away from gambling. Consider the very popular casino game "craps." One

Table 4.1 All possible pairs from simultaneously rolling two dice.

	1	2	3	4	5	6
1	1,1	1,2	1,3	1,4	1,5	1,6
2	2,1	2,2	2,3	2,4	2,5	2,6
3	3,1	3,2	3,3	3,4	3,5	3,6
4	4,1	4,2	4,3	4,4	4,5	4,6
5	5,1	5,2	5,3	5,4	5,5	5,6
6	6,1	6,2	6,3	6,4	6,5	6,6

of the simplest bets in this game is called the Pass. You throw two dice. If your dice sum to 7 or 11, then you win (the casino matches your bet). So, what are the chances of winning the Pass with a 7 or an 11? We already know the probability of rolling a 7 is 6/36. So, if we add another possibility that can allow us to win the Pass, it must be the case that the probability of winning is greater than 6/36. Once we figure out the probability of rolling an 11, then we can add them together to determine the probability of winning. How many ways can we roll an 11? The only combination that adds to 11 is 5 and 6, and there are two ways that can occur. So, the probability of rolling an 11 is 2/36. Putting it all together, the probability of rolling a 7 or 11 is = 6/36 + 2/36 = 8/36. So, about 22% of the time (a bit more than 1 in every 5 turns) you could expect to win the Pass in craps.

Note that we added probabilities in the previous example. We added the probabilities because the question was an *or* question. When you see the term *or* in probability questions that means you are going to be adding probabilities. What is the probability it rains *or* it does not rain today? This question requires adding both probabilities together. Even without having any idea of the actual probability of it raining, we know the answer must be 1 because of two reasons. There are only two possible outcomes (it rains or it does not) and they are mutually exclusive, so they add to one. Statisticians, just to confuse things, use the term *union* to describe adding the probability of multiple events. For example, the probability of rolling a 7 or 11 can also be described as the probability of the union of 7 and 11 (see Formula A.4).

Let us get some more practice before we move on to a different type of probability. We are still rolling two dice, but this time we do not care about the sum of the two numbers. Rather, we are interested in the individual result of each of the two dice. What is the probability you roll either a 2 *or* a 3 on either die? As before, we will add the probabilities of each separate outcome. However, this time, we have to be careful not to double count the instances in which a 2 and 3 are rolled together. This is because rolling a 2 or rolling a 3 are not mutually exclusive. Rolling a 2 does not exclude the possibility of rolling a 3 on the other die. Since there are 36 possible outcomes, we can still refer to Table 4.1. Let us first consider the cases in which a 2 is rolled. These possibilities are contained in Table 4.2.

There are 11 different ways of getting a two from rolling two dice, therefore the probability of rolling at least one 2 is 11/36. The question, however, asked about the probability of rolling a 2 *or* a 3. All of the instances in which a 3 is rolled on two dice can be found in Table 4.3.

There are also 11 instances in which a three is rolled on either die. So, the probability of rolling a three is also 11/36. Now, to compute the probability of rolling a 2 or a 3, we want to add the probabilities of the individual events, but we must remember to subtract the cases that overlap. We cannot double count. Comparing Table 4.2 with Table 4.3, we can see there are two instances

Table 4.2 Rolling a 2 from a pair of dice.

	1	2	3	4	5	6
1		1,2				
2	2,1	2,2	2,3	2,4	2,5	2,6
3		3,2				
4		4,2				
5		5,2				
6		6,2				

Table 4.3 Rolling a 3 from a pair of dice.

	1	2	3	4	5	6
1			1,3			
2			2,3			
3	3,1	3,2	3,3	3,4	3,5	3,6
4			4,3			
5			5,3			
6			6,3			

of overlap. Therefore, the probability of rolling a two or a three is $11/36 + 11/36 - 2/36 = 20/36$ or $5/9$. The places where they overlap are called *intersections*.

4.1.2 When to Find Intersections

When probability questions have the word *and* that indicates you will need to find intersections. From the previous example, if the equation was to find the probability of rolling a 2 *and* a 3, then there are only two instances in which this outcome can occur. It is the intersection of 2 and 3, and the probability is therefore $2/36 = 1/18$. Notice that this probability is much smaller than the probability of rolling a 2 *or* a 3.

Consider a standard deck of 52 playing cards. In case you too shy away from card playing and gambling, there are four of each number card and four of each face card in a deck, two black (spades and clubs) and two red (diamonds and hearts). First, suppose I am interested in finding the probability of drawing one card and it being red. Since half of the cards in the deck are red, the probability is $26/52$. Now, let us say I am interested in the probability of drawing a card that is red *and* it is an Ace. In this case, we are interested in the intersection of the Aces and red cards. There are only two red cards that are Aces, so the probability of

Figure 4.2 Venn diagram showing the intersection for drawing either an Ace or a Red card.

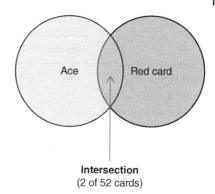

Intersection
(2 of 52 cards)

the intersection is 2/52. This intersection is illustrated in the *Venn diagram* in Figure 4.2.

What about the probability of drawing a single card that is either red *or* an Ace? There are 26 red cards and 4 Ace cards. However, two of the four Aces are red cards. That is, red cards and Ace cards are not mutually exclusive (they can both occur with a single draw of a card). So, when we find probabilities that are unions (those *or* probabilities), we must remember to subtract the intersections. If we did not, we would be double counting cards. Therefore, the number of unique cards that are either red or an Ace are $26 + 4 - 2 = 28$. The probability is therefore $28/52 = 0.5385$.

4.2 Empirical Probabilities

When the *Titanic* collided with an iceberg on her maiden voyage in April of 1912, the likelihood of surviving the wreck was not the same for all passengers. Women and children, for instance, were given preference to board emergency raft boats. It turns out that class also affected the probability of survival. In this section, we will use the historic data of *Titanic* survivors to explore probabilities that are calculated based on the observed outcomes. This is called the *empirical* or the *relative frequency* approach to finding probabilities. With empirical probabilities, we simply let the data do the talking. For our example, the passengers and crew aboard the *Titanic* are displayed in Table 4.4. Table 4.4 is an example of what is called a *contingency table*, which is a cross-tabulation of frequencies for a set of events.

Table 4.4 shows that 2224 people were aboard the ship on its voyage across the Atlantic. There were both passengers and crew aboard segmented by men, women, and children. The passengers are further divided into three classes. Using the same categories, Table 4.5 shows the number of people who were saved and survived the shipwreck.

Table 4.4 *Titanic* passengers and crew.

	Men	Women	Children	Total
First class	175	144	6	325
Second class	168	93	24	285
Third class	462	165	79	706
Crew	885	23	–	908
Total	1690	425	109	2224

Table 4.5 *Titanic* survivors.

	Men	Women	Children	Total
First class	57	140	6	203
Second class	14	80	24	118
Third class	75	76	27	178
Crew	192	20	–	212
Total	338	316	57	711

From Table 4.5, we see that 711 people survived the sinking of the *Titanic*. Let us start with a broad question. What was the probability of a person aboard the *Titanic* surviving? To answer this empirical probability question, we need to calculate the relative frequency of survivors. This is simply the number that survived divided by the total number onboard $= 711/2224 = 0.3197$. So, without conditioning the question on the characteristic of the passenger or crew, we can say that a person in general had slightly less than a one in three chance of survival. However, not all groups had an equal chance of survival. To illustrate this, consider the probability of a child surviving the wreck. In total, there were 109 children onboard and 57 of them were saved. So, the chance of surviving the wreck *given* that the passenger was a child was $57/109 = 0.5229$. What about the chance of survival for a passenger who was a child *and* that passenger was in first class? This probability is found at the intersection of children and first class. We can see that 6 of 6 survived, so the probability was equal to 1.

Now consider the probability of surviving if the person was a woman *or* a child. From Table 4.5, we see that 316 women survived and 57 children survived, so the total number is $316 + 57 = 373$. From Table 4.4, we see that there were 425 women and 109 children onboard, with a total of $425 + 109 = 534$. So, the probability of survival for a woman or a child was $373/534 = 0.6985$, which is a bit more than a 2 in 3 chance.

These probability examples are called *conditional probabilities*, which are probabilities of events occurring given that something else has occurred. In

Table 4.6 Conditional probabilities of surviving the *Titanic's* maiden voyage.

	Men	Women	Children	Combined
First class	0.3257	0.9722	1.0000	0.6246
Second class	0.0833	0.8602	1.0000	0.4140
Third class	0.1623	0.4606	0.3418	0.2521
Crew	0.2169	0.8696	–	0.2335
Combined	0.2000	0.7435	0.5229	0.3197

many problems in statistics, it is the word "given" that indicates you need to find a conditional probability. For example, what is the probability of survival for a male passenger, *given* that he had a first class ticket? The denominator of the calculation is the given part, which is the subset of the men who had first class tickets (175 passengers). The numerator is the number of men who survived who were first class passengers (57). So, the probability of surviving the shipwreck for a man, given he had a first class ticket was $57/175 = 0.3257$. All of the probabilities of survival conditional on the intersection of passenger class and whether a male, female, or child are displayed in Table 4.6. The probabilities are computed by dividing the cells in Table 4.5 by the corresponding cells in Table 4.4. As an example, 0.3257 – the probability of survival for a male, first-class ticket holder – is found in the upper-left corner. The Table is useful for making quick comparisons of conditional probabilities. For example, we see that the probability of survival for a child passenger with a first or second class ticket is much higher than for a child in the third class. Also, males and females had a better chance of survival if they held first class tickets compared to other ticket classes.

4.3 Conditional Probabilities

Having a good understanding of conditional probabilities is useful for thinking critically about some of the statistics you are confronted with every day. Statistics can often be misleading if they are based on a large population of people when in reality they should be focused on only a subset. About 610,000 people die of heart disease in the United States each year.[1] That boils down to one in every four deaths, or an empirical probability of 0.25. Does that suggest that everyone should expect a one in four chance of dying from heart disease? No. This statistic pools everyone together, combining all of the people who are at

---

1 https://www.cdc.gov/heartdisease/facts.htm

high risk (e.g., obese and smokers) with those that are at low risk (e.g., healthy weight and nonsmokers). The conditional probabilities would be different. An obese smoker's chance of dying from heart disease is much higher than 0.25 and the healthy person's chance is much lower.

A good example of how conditional probabilities can be misinterpreted is presented in a study by Krämer and Gigerenzer.[2] They consider the question: "What is the probability that a woman with a positive mammography result actually has cancer?" They report that the probability of a woman having breast cancer is 0.008, and if she has breast cancer, the test will show a positive result 90% of the time. The test, in other words, is 90% accurate in terms of detecting cancer that is present. However, if a woman does not have breast cancer, the test will reveal that she does 7% of the time. Given these statistics, what is the probability that a woman who has a positive test result actually has cancer?

In a study of 24 experienced doctors that were provided with this information, 22 answered incorrectly. Most answered that if the woman tests positive, there is a 90% chance she has cancer. They were simply reporting the accuracy of the test at detecting cancer if a patient has cancer. They ignored all of the women who would test positive even if they did not have cancer. Those 7% false positives. So, what is the probability that the woman with a positive test result actually has cancer?

Let us work through it using a contingency table (Table 4.7). From experience, the simplest way to work through these problems is to start with an example population size and fill in the table with the frequencies in each cell. Consider an example population of 10,000 women. Of the 10,000, only 80 women will have cancer (i.e., 10,000 × 0.008), and this value is found in the "Total" column in the "Has cancer" row. Now, of those 80, 90% will be accurately diagnosed, which yields 72 positive results and 8 negative results. Of the 9920 women who do not have cancer, 7% of them will be told that they do. This results in 694 woman receiving false positives. Therefore, 72 + 694 = 766 is the total number of women who receive a positive test result. Given a positive test result, only 72 will actually have cancer, which means the probability that a woman has cancer, given that she tests positive, is 72/766 = 0.094. Less than 10%. Only two

Table 4.7 Contingency table of cancer prevalence and test results.

	Positive test result	Negative test result	Total
Has cancer	72	8	80
Does not have cancer	694	9226	9920
Total	766	9234	10000

2 Krämer, W. and G. Gigerenzer. (2005) "How to confuse with statistics or: The use and misuse of conditional probabilities." Statistical Science 20(3):223–230.

doctors who participated in the study answered correctly. While most doctors thought the woman in question had a 90% chance of having cancer in reality it was fairly unlikely that she did. This type of careless thinking is not trivial. Many patients have been given poor advice about medical care by doctors who do not understand how to interpret statistics.

You may have heard the adage that most vehicle accidents occur within three miles of people's homes. While this is likely true, it is not because driving is more dangerous when we are closer to home. It is just that most trips people take are short, and with more trips it is unsurprising we observe a higher frequency of accidents. However, the probability of an accident occurring within three miles from home is likely not higher compared to trips beyond the three mile range. It is all about conditioning the analysis on the relevant events. Both the medical example and the accident example highlight that conditional probabilities do not work the same both ways. The probability of testing positive, *given* the patient has cancer is 0.90, while the probability of having cancer, *given* the patient tested positive is 0.094. Totally different. Likewise, the probability of getting into an accident, *given* that the driver is within three miles from home is different from the probability that the driver is three miles from home, *given* that she got into an accident.

4.4 Summary

Every undergraduate textbook in business statistics has a chapter on probability. In other words, the probability of an undergraduate stats book having a chapter on probability = 1.0. Apart from the difficulty many students have with understanding probabilities, the chapter is often a bit disjointed from the rest of the text. It usually follows chapters on sampling techniques and descriptive statistics and it is not immediately obvious where it fits in. However, the chapter on probability is a gateway into the world of inferential statistics. Understanding probabilities is key to understanding how we use sample data to infer unknown characteristics regarding a population. Random samples lead to sample statistics that have their own distribution, and those distributions define the probabilities of all possible outcomes. We turn to the most important probability distribution – the normal distribution – in Chapter 5.

The objective of this chapter was to offer an intuitive approach to understanding simple (or classical) and empirical probabilities. Examples of coin flips, die rolls, and draws from a deck of cards were used to illustrate the concepts of simple probabilities. We turned again to data from the *Titanic* to illustrate empirical probabilities – those that are calculated using observed frequencies of certain events occurring. We will rely on both simple and empirical probabilities in the upcoming chapters on inferential statistics.

Technical Appendix

For any event A, it must be the case that the probability of the event is no greater than one and no less than zero. Notationally, we can write this as

$$0 \leq P(A) \leq 1, \tag{A.1}$$

where P indicates probability.

If we let S denote the entire sample space of simple events, then it must be the case that

$$P(S) = 1. \tag{A.2}$$

For an event A, if we denote the collection of all other events as A^c, then the *Complement Rule* states

$$P(A^c) = 1 - P(A), \tag{A.3}$$

which follows directly from the fact that $P(S) = 1$.

The probability of a union (an *or* probability) is computed using formula A.4 below. Formula A.4 is often referred to as the *General Law of Addition*. The notation $\cup$ indicates a union and the notation $\cap$ indicates an intersection (an *and* probability).

$$P(A \cup B) = P(A) + P(B) - P(A \cap B) \tag{A.4}$$

Note that if events A and B are mutually exclusive, then $P(A \cap B) = 0$, and this special case is called the *Special Law of Addition*.

To calculate the probability of an event, *given* that another event occurs, we use the *conditional probability formula*

$$P(A|B) = \frac{P(A \cap B)}{P(B)}, \tag{A.5}$$

where the term $|$ means *given*.

The *General Law of Multiplication* – used to determine joint probabilities and intersections – is the following:

$$P(A \cap B) = P(A|B)P(B), \tag{A.6}$$

and if events A and B are independent, then $P(A \cap B) = P(A)P(B)$, which is the *Special Law of Multiplication*.

5

The Normal Distribution

Only a textbook in statistics could get away with entitling a chapter "The Normal Distribution." If you thought that the topic of distributions was less than exciting, then what chance does a *normal* one have? No matter how hard you try you cannot get away from the *normal distribution*. Every time you see the results of a political poll in the news, those results are based on the normal distribution. The findings from most scientific studies – from those telling you that you need more exercise to those bragging their batteries last the longest – all rely on the normal distribution. In this chapter, we will consider attributes of datasets that are distributed normally. While it is true that some data are naturally known to be normally distributed, the real usefulness of the normal distribution starts in Chapter 6 on sampling distributions. However, before we get there, we need to know the fundamentals, and introducing those fundamentals is the goal of this chapter. The normal distribution is a *continuous probability distribution*, implying that the underlying data are continuous. Recall, continuous data can take on any value within a range (i.e., fractions make sense). As we will find out later, however, sometimes even discrete data can be safely *approximated* as normal.

5.1 The Bell Shape

The normal distribution is probably best described as a "bell-shaped" distribution. Some textbooks call it "mound shaped." Fancier textbooks call it "Gaussian", named after German mathematician Karl Gauss (1777–1855). Sometimes, students have a hard time grasping the concept that data have a shape. A useful visual, even if it is just made mentally, is a histogram of data. Recall, on the horizontal axis of a histogram are the ranges of values of the data (called bins) and the vertical axis either has the frequency (total number) in each bin or the relative frequency (total number in a bin divided by the total observations) in each bin. The normal distribution is symmetric and so the part of the distribution less than the mean is the mirror image of the part of

A Guide to Business Statistics, First Edition. David M. McEvoy.
© 2018 John Wiley & Sons, Inc. Published 2018 by John Wiley & Sons, Inc.

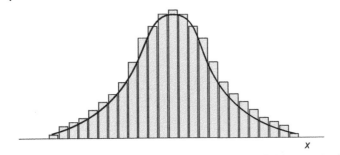

x

Figure 5.1 The figure illustrates a smooth normal distribution (dark line) drawn over a histogram of data for a variable x.

the distribution greater than the mean. Recall from Chapter 3 on descriptive statistics that symmetry implies that the mean equals the median. In fact, with the normal distribution, we can say: *mean = median = mode.* The normal distribution is a continuous distribution and is most often represented by a smooth line like the one in Figure 5.1. While there are other distributions that are mound shaped (the *t*-distribution for example), the normal distribution has some particularly unique properties. These properties are outlined in what is called the *Empirical Rule.*

5.2 The Empirical Rule

The Empirical Rule has much in common with Chebyshev's theorem. We cannot forget Chebyshev. Remember that Chebyshev's formula was used to get a lower-bound estimate of how much data is within k standard deviations around the mean for any dataset with any shape. However, if we know that the distribution of data is normal, then we can be more precise. The Empirical Rule – illustrated in Figure 5.2 – says that if a dataset is normal, then it must be the case that:

- roughly 68% of the data will be within one standard deviation around the mean ("around" meaning the range from one standard deviation below the mean to one standard deviation above the mean)
- roughly 95% of the data will be within two standard deviations around the mean
- roughly 99.7% of the data will be within three standard deviations around the mean

The z label on the horizontal axis in Figure 5.2 denotes the number of standard deviations away from the mean for the variable x. Right away, we observe that the Empirical Rule gives us more useful information than Chebyshev's formula. Recall from Chapter 3 that Chebyshev's formula estimated that at least

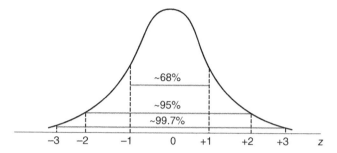

Figure 5.2 The Empirical Rule for normally distributed data.

75% of data is found within two standard deviations of the mean. Of course, this is true of any distribution, including the normal one. However, with the normal distribution by the Empirical Rule, we can say that approximately 95% of the data is within the same numeric range. Note that almost all data lie within three standard deviations. So, if a dataset is normal, the chance of a single data point being outside of three standard deviations (either greater than or less than) is about 0.03% (100 − 99.7%). In other words, it would be extremely rare. The concept of rare events defined by the number of standard deviations away from the mean will come up again later.

Let us get some practice using the Empirical Rule. The average height of an adult American male is roughly 69 inches with a standard deviation of 3 inches. Population data on height are typically normally distributed, so it is safe to assume this is the case.

Question: What percentage of American men are between 63 and 75 inches tall?

We need to determine how many standard deviations 63 and 75 are from the mean. With a standard deviation of 3 inches, it should be clear that 63 inches is two standard deviations below the mean (i.e., $69 − 2 \times 3 = 63$) and 75 inches is two standard deviations above the mean. By the second element of the Empirical Rule, we know that about 95% of all men will be between 63 and 75 inches tall. In other words, of the American men reading this book, only about 5% will either be shorter than 63 inches *or* taller than 75 inches.

There is another very useful way to think about the Empirical Rule. Consider the first bullet point, stating that 68% of all the data can be found within one standard deviation around the mean. This also implies that if we randomly chose a single value from the entire distribution, the *chance* or *probability* that value is within one standard deviation of the mean is $68/100 = 0.68$. Therefore, the Empirical Rule can be rewritten in probability terms. For any normally distributed dataset:

- the probability of a randomly selected value falling within one standard deviation around the mean is roughly *0.68*.

- the probability of a randomly selected value falling within two standard deviation around the mean is roughly *0.95*.
- the probability of a randomly selected value falling within three standard deviations of the mean is roughly *0.997*.

5.3   Standard Normal Distribution

The Empirical Rule is useful for getting a feel for how dispersed a normally distributed dataset is, but it has its limitations. Consider again the average adult American male with a height of 69 inches and a standard deviation of 3 inches. What percentage of men is between 67 and 71 inches tall? Or, in probability terms, we can ask:

> **Question:** what is the probability that a randomly selected American adult male is between 67 and 71 inches tall?

To answer this question, we have to look beyond the Empirical Rule because the distances from the mean in standard deviations are not integer values. Clearly, 67 inches is less than one standard deviation from the mean of 69 (note, one standard deviation below the mean is $69 - 3 = 66$). To answer this question, we turn to what is called the *standard normal distribution*. Every value from a normally distributed dataset can be transformed into a standardized value simply by subtracting the mean and dividing by the standard deviation (see Formula A.1). We call this a z-score. The z-score tells us how many standard deviations a value is away from the mean. The standard normal distribution, also known as the z distribution, has a mean of zero and a standard deviation of 1. The distribution in Figure 5.2 is the standard normal distribution. The graph of the standard normal distribution typically ranges from -3 to $+3$ standard deviations (remember, from the Empirical Rule just about all of the data are within this range).

Returning back to our question, the z-score can tell us how many standard deviations an American male with a height of 67 inches is from the average of 69. This is $(67-69)/3 = -2/3$, which means that a man 67 inches tall is 0.67 standard deviations *less than* the average man. Likewise, a man 71 inches tall is 0.67 standard deviations *greater than* the average man (i.e., $(71-69)/3 = 2/3$). This area is illustrated in Figure 5.3.

To find the probability of a man being between 67 and 71 inches tall, we need to take these z-scores to what is called the *standard normal table* or more informally the *z-table*. A few different versions of the standard normal table are available in most textbooks. One version of the table makes use of the fact that the left-hand side is the mirror image of the right-hand side for a normal distribution, and only includes positive z-scores (only the right-hand side of the

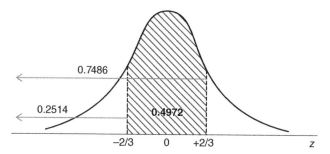

Figure 5.3 Beyond the Empirical Rule: Finding an area under the normal distribution.

z	0.00	0.01	0.02	0.03	0.04	0.05	0.06	0.07	0.08	0.09
0.0	0.5000	0.5040	0.5080	0.5120	0.5160	0.5199	0.5239	0.5279	0.5319	0.5359
0.1	0.5398	0.5438	0.5478	0.5517	0.5557	0.5596	0.5636	0.5675	0.5714	0.5753
0.2	0.5793	0.5832	0.5871	0.5910	0.5948	0.5987	0.6026	0.6064	0.6103	0.6141
0.3	0.6179	0.6217	0.6255	0.6293	0.6331	0.6368	0.6406	0.6443	0.6480	0.6517
0.4	0.6554	0.6591	0.6628	0.6664	0.6700	0.6736	0.6772	0.6808	0.6844	0.6879
0.5	0.6915	0.6950	0.6985	0.7019	0.7054	0.7088	0.7123	0.7157	0.7190	0.7224
0.6	0.7257	0.7291	0.7324	0.7357	0.7389	0.7422	0.7454	0.7486	0.7517	0.7549
0.7	0.7580	0.7611	0.7642	0.7673	0.7704	0.7734	0.7764	0.7794	0.7823	0.7852
0.8	0.7881	0.7910	0.7939	0.7967	0.7995	0.8023	0.8051	0.8078	0.8106	0.8133
0.9	0.8159	0.8186	0.8212	0.8238	0.8264	0.8289	0.8315	0.8340	0.8365	0.8389
1.0	0.8413	0.8438	0.8461	0.8485	0.8508	0.8531	0.8554	0.8577	0.8599	0.8621

Figure 5.4 A section of the cumulative z-table.

distribution). The other type of table includes both sides. We call this the *cumulative standard normal table*, and this is the one we will refer to in this text (see Table 5.1 in the Technical Appendix). You can use any z-table you want because if you use them correctly you will get the same answer regardless of the format.

Rule: any z-value you look up on the cumulative z-table gives you the entire area (probability) to the *left* of that z-value.

Figure 5.4 contains just a small section of the positive side of the cumulative z-table. The first column has the z values to the first decimal place. The top row has the second decimal place. Note that $z = 0.00$ is the mean value and the area to the left of the mean is always 0.50. When we look up $2/3 = 0.67$ on the table, it tells us that the area to the left is 0.7486 (highlighted with a shaded box). In other words, the probability of an adult male with a height of 71 inches or less is 0.7486 (about 75% of the population). Now, to find the probability of a male being between 67 inches and 71 inches, we have to subtract the area to the left of 67 inches. What is that area? Simply look up $-2/3 = -0.67$ on the table and find 0.2514. Or alternatively, recognizing the symmetry of the normal distribution, that area will be equal to $1 - 0.7486 = 0.2514$. So, the area between 67 and 71 inches is $0.7486 - 0.2514 = 0.4972$. To wrap it up, we can say that the probability of an adult male being between 67 and 71 inches tall is 0.4972. This area is illustrated in Figure 5.3.

It is important to reiterate that this technique can be used to find probabilities for any normally distributed dataset. Simply find the z-values and go to the table. The area you get is the probability of getting a z value *less than* the one you looked up.

5.3.1 Probabilities with Continuous Distributions

The previous example led us to calculate the probability that a randomly chosen adult male is between 67 and 71 inches tall. That is, we found a probability of a person being within a certain *range* for the continuous dataset on height. What if we wanted to find the probability of randomly selecting an adult male who is, for example, exactly 67 inches tall? The answer to this question is effectively zero. When data are continuous, or approximately continuous, then there are effectively an infinite number of possible values the variable can take. Given our example on height, someone may be 67.0001 inches tall, while another person may be 67.543 inches tall. Remember, continuous data are not countable. Fractions make sense. So, when there are effectively infinite possibilities, then the probability of one exact event occurring is approximated by $1/\infty = 0$. The point is, we always find probabilities within a range of values when data are continuous.

5.3.2 Verifying the Empirical Rule Using the z-table

To get more practice using the cumulative z-table, we can use the table to verify the three parts to the Empirical Rule. The first part of the Empirical Rule states that the probability of a value falling within one standard deviation of the mean in either direction is 0.68. If we look up a positive $z = 1$ on the table (see Figure 5.4 or Table 5.1), we get a probability of 0.8413. That is, the area of everything to the left of $z = 1.0$. From 0.8413, we must subtract the area less than $z = -1.0$, which from the table is 0.1587. Therefore, from the z-table, the area within one standard deviation of the mean is $0.8413 - 0.1587 = 0.6826$. Thus, we confirm the first aspect of the Empirical Rule that the probability is approximately 0.68.

We can do the same for the other two parts of the Empirical Rule. From the z-table, the probability of a normally distributed value falling within two standard deviations of the mean is $0.9772 - 0.0228 = 0.9544$, or roughly 0.95. Finally, the probability of a normally distributed value falling within three standard deviations of the mean is $0.9987 - 0.0013 = 0.9974$.

5.4 Normal Approximations

So far, in this chapter, we have considered continuous variables that happen to be normally distributed. It turns out that in some situations data that are not continuous can be safely approximated as normal distributions. One of the most important cases is the *binomial distribution.* The binomial distribution arises from categorical data that can be coded in binary form (i.e., 0 or 1). Examples are flipping a coin (heads or tails), tax audits (audited or not audited), and voting (voted for a candidate or did not vote for a candidate). The two events must be mutually exclusive (both cannot occur at once) and all inclusive (cover all possibilities). Typically, the event marked with a 1 is called a "success" and the event marked with a "0" is a failure. In this context, the terms success and failure do not imply anything about the relative merits of the two events, it is just a point of reference. The binomial distribution is the collection of all possible "successes" that could occur from a given number of *trials.* You can think of a trial as the action being taken. Each flip of a coin, each roll of a die, each audit, and each vote is a trial. Suppose, we flipped a coin 50 times and each flip recorded a 1 if we got a heads (a success) or a 0 if we got a tails (a failure). The collection of all possible successes from those 50 flips is a binomial distribution. For the distribution to be binomial, the probability of a success (or failure) for each trial must be independent of previous trials. The example of flipping a coin is intuitive; that is, the probability of landing a heads is 0.50 independent of what occurred on any previous flips. However, if the trial is randomly choosing a voter to determine whether or not they voted for a particular candidate, for the distribution to be binomial the likelihood each voter is chosen must be the same for each trial.[1] Like any distribution of data, the binomial distribution can be characterized by its *mean, standard deviation,* and *shape.*

5.4.1 Mean

The mean of the binomial distribution, also called the *expected value,* is simply the number of trials × the probability of a success. How many heads do you expect to get from 50 flips of a coin? You can probably answer 25 just using your intuition; that is, half of the time you should expect to get a heads. We use the Greek letter π to denote the probability of a success, and therefore $1 - \pi$ is the probability of a failure. The number of trials is denoted as n. So, the mean of the binomial distribution is $\mu = n\pi$.

5.4.2 Standard deviation

Although we might expect 25 heads from 50 flips of a coin, we are well aware that we might not get 25 heads exactly. In fact, it is possible, although highly improbable, that we get zero heads from 50 flips of a coin. The point is that there will be variation in the number of successes you get from 50 flips of a coin.

---

1 Trials that meet the criteria to form a binomial distribution are often called Bernoulli trials (or the experiment follows the Bernoulli process).

How much variation? The variance of the binomial distribution is the expected number of successes × the probability of a failure. The standard deviation, as in Chapter 3, is simply the square root of the variance. The standard deviation can be interpreted as the average deviation from the expected value. For our example, it is the average deviation from the expected 25 heads, and equals 3.54 heads (see Formula A.3).

5.4.3 Shape

What shape does a binomial distribution take? It turns out that if the number of trials is large enough, then we can safely approximate the binomial distribution as normal. How many trials are required? As long as $n\pi$ and $n(1-\pi)$ are both at least 10, then we can say that the distribution of successes is normal (see Formula A.2). That is, it has the familiar bell shape. This is great news. Given that it is normal, we can rely on the Empirical Rule and the z-table to find probabilities of specific events. Remember, any normally distributed variable can be converted into a z-score and looked up on the z-table. Formula A.4 shows how to find a z-score for any binomial distribution that can be approximated as normal.

Consider again the distribution of heads for 50 flips of a coin. The distribution can be safely approximated as normal because $n\pi = n(1-\pi) = 25$. The mean of the distribution is 25 heads and the standard deviation is 3.54 heads.

Question: what is the probability that we get 30 heads or less when flipping a coin 50 times?

The distribution of heads for 50 coin flips is illustrated in Figure 5.5. The variable x denotes the number of heads. The standard deviations have been rounded to one decimal place to simplify the graph. To answer the question, we need to find the z-score for 30 heads and then go to the z table to find the area. The

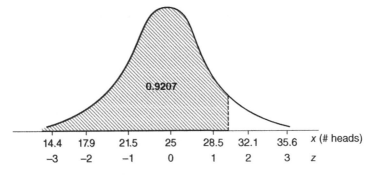

Figure 5.5 Probability of getting 30 heads or less from 50 flips of a coin.

z-score is simply the difference between 30 and the expected 25 over the standard deviation. Therefore, $z = (30 − 25)/3.54 = 1.41$; that is, 30 is 1.41 standard deviations away from 25. If we look up 1.41 on the z-table, it gives us 0.9207. In other words, the probability of getting 30 heads or less from 50 flips is 0.9207.

5.5 Summary

This chapter was dedicated to normally distributed data. These data are symmetric and bell shaped. We learned how to standardize any normally distributed variable by finding the z-score. The z-score tells us how many standard deviations x is from the mean. The normal distribution is a specific type of continuous probability distribution. There are many other continuous probability distributions, including the uniform distribution, the exponential distribution, and the triangular distribution. However, most of the tools we learn for inferential statistics (including hypothesis testing and regression in the coming chapters) rely on assumptions of normality. For this reason, this chapter is uniquely focused on helping students understand the normal distribution. We considered populations of continuous data that are normally distributed (close examples include data on height, sleep patterns, and shoe size). We also considered distributions of binary data that can be approximated as normal. Examples here included flipping a coin and rolling a die. However, the real value in understanding normal data is revealed in the next chapter on sampling distributions. It turns out that even if population datasets are dramatically skewed, the distributions formed from taking samples from those populations are often normal.

Technical Appendix

Any normally distributed variable can be converted into a *z-score*. We call this process "standardizing" the data. For a continuous variable x, the formula is:

$$z = \frac{x - \mu}{\sigma}, \tag{A.1}$$

where μ is the population mean and σ is the population standard deviation. The z-score tells you how many standard deviations the x value is from its mean.

The binomial distribution (think binary data) can be *approximated as normal* provided that both of the following conditions hold:

$$n\pi \geq 10$$
$$n(1 - \pi) \geq 10, \tag{A.2}$$

where π is the probability of a success (a success is a 1 in a sample of binary data) and $(1 - \pi)$ is the probability of a failure (a 0 in the data), and n is the number of trials. The *expected number* of successes is $n\pi$. The standard deviation of the binomial distribution is:

$$\sigma = \sqrt{n\pi(1 - \pi)}. \tag{A.3}$$

To standardize x number of successes for a normally approximated binomial distribution, we use the following:

$$z = \frac{x - n\pi}{\sqrt{n\pi(1 - \pi)}}. \tag{A.4}$$

Table 5.1a Cumulative standard normal table – negative *z*-scores.

z	0.09	0.08	0.07	0.06	0.05	0.04	0.03	0.02	0.01	0.00
−3.9	0.0001	0.0001	0.0001	0.0001	0.0001	0.0001	0.0001	0.0001	0.0001	0.0000
−3.8	0.0001	0.0001	0.0001	0.0001	0.0001	0.0001	0.0001	0.0001	0.0001	0.0001
−3.7	0.0002	0.0001	0.0001	0.0001	0.0001	0.0001	0.0001	0.0001	0.0001	0.0001
−3.6	0.0002	0.0002	0.0002	0.0002	0.0002	0.0002	0.0002	0.0002	0.0002	0.0002
−3.5	0.0003	0.0003	0.0003	0.0003	0.0003	0.0003	0.0003	0.0003	0.0002	0.0002
−3.4	0.0005	0.0005	0.0004	0.0004	0.0004	0.0004	0.0004	0.0004	0.0003	0.0003
−3.3	0.0007	0.0006	0.0006	0.0006	0.0006	0.0006	0.0005	0.0005	0.0005	0.0005
−3.2	0.0009	0.0009	0.0009	0.0008	0.0008	0.0008	0.0008	0.0007	0.0007	0.0007
−3.1	0.0013	0.0013	0.0012	0.0012	0.0011	0.0011	0.0011	0.0010	0.0010	0.0010
−3.0	0.0018	0.0018	0.0017	0.0016	0.0016	0.0015	0.0015	0.0014	0.0014	0.0013
−2.9	0.0025	0.0024	0.0023	0.0023	0.0022	0.0021	0.0021	0.0020	0.0019	0.0019
−2.8	0.0034	0.0033	0.0032	0.0031	0.0030	0.0029	0.0028	0.0027	0.0026	0.0026
−2.7	0.0045	0.0044	0.0043	0.0041	0.0040	0.0039	0.0038	0.0037	0.0036	0.0035
−2.6	0.0060	0.0059	0.0057	0.0055	0.0054	0.0052	0.0051	0.0049	0.0048	0.0047
−2.5	0.0080	0.0078	0.0075	0.0073	0.0071	0.0069	0.0068	0.0066	0.0064	0.0062
−2.4	0.0104	0.0102	0.0099	0.0096	0.0094	0.0091	0.0089	0.0087	0.0084	0.0082
−2.3	0.0136	0.0132	0.0129	0.0125	0.0122	0.0119	0.0116	0.0113	0.0110	0.0107
−2.2	0.0174	0.0170	0.0166	0.0162	0.0158	0.0154	0.0150	0.0146	0.0143	0.0139
−2.1	0.0222	0.0217	0.0212	0.0207	0.0202	0.0197	0.0192	0.0188	0.0183	0.0179
−2.0	0.0281	0.0274	0.0268	0.0262	0.0256	0.0250	0.0244	0.0239	0.0233	0.0228
−1.9	0.0351	0.0344	0.0336	0.0329	0.0322	0.0314	0.0307	0.0301	0.0294	0.0287
−1.8	0.0436	0.0427	0.0418	0.0409	0.0401	0.0392	0.0384	0.0375	0.0367	0.0359
−1.7	0.0537	0.0526	0.0516	0.0505	0.0495	0.0485	0.0475	0.0465	0.0455	0.0446
−1.6	0.0655	0.0643	0.0630	0.0618	0.0606	0.0594	0.0582	0.0571	0.0559	0.0548
−1.5	0.0793	0.0778	0.0764	0.0749	0.0735	0.0721	0.0708	0.0694	0.0681	0.0668
−1.4	0.0951	0.0934	0.0918	0.0901	0.0885	0.0869	0.0853	0.0838	0.0823	0.0808
−1.3	0.1131	0.1112	0.1093	0.1075	0.1056	0.1038	0.1020	0.1003	0.0985	0.0968
−1.2	0.1335	0.1314	0.1292	0.1271	0.1251	0.1230	0.1210	0.1190	0.1170	0.1151
−1.1	0.1562	0.1539	0.1515	0.1492	0.1469	0.1446	0.1423	0.1401	0.1379	0.1357
−1.0	0.1814	0.1788	0.1762	0.1736	0.1711	0.1685	0.1660	0.1635	0.1611	0.1587
−0.9	0.2090	0.2061	0.2033	0.2005	0.1977	0.1949	0.1922	0.1894	0.1867	0.1841
−0.8	0.2389	0.2358	0.2327	0.2296	0.2266	0.2236	0.2206	0.2177	0.2148	0.2119
−0.7	0.2709	0.2676	0.2643	0.2611	0.2578	0.2546	0.2514	0.2483	0.2451	0.2420
−0.6	0.3050	0.3015	0.2981	0.2946	0.2912	0.2877	0.2843	0.2810	0.2776	0.2743
−0.5	0.3409	0.3372	0.3336	0.3300	0.3264	0.3228	0.3192	0.3156	0.3121	0.3085
−0.4	0.3783	0.3745	0.3707	0.3669	0.3632	0.3594	0.3557	0.3520	0.3483	0.3446
−0.3	0.4168	0.4129	0.4090	0.4052	0.4013	0.3974	0.3936	0.3897	0.3859	0.3821
−0.2	0.4562	0.4522	0.4483	0.4443	0.4404	0.4364	0.4325	0.4286	0.4247	0.4207
−0.1	0.4960	0.4920	0.4880	0.4840	0.4801	0.4761	0.4721	0.4681	0.4641	0.4602
−0.0	0.5359	0.5319	0.5279	0.5239	0.5199	0.5160	0.5120	0.5080	0.5040	0.5000

Table 5.1b Cumulative standard normal table – positive *z*-scores.

z	0.00	0.01	0.02	0.03	0.04	0.05	0.06	0.07	0.08	0.09
0.0	0.5000	0.5040	0.5080	0.5120	0.5160	0.5199	0.5239	0.5279	0.5319	0.5359
0.1	0.5398	0.5438	0.5478	0.5517	0.5557	0.5596	0.5636	0.5675	0.5714	0.5753
0.2	0.5793	0.5832	0.5871	0.5910	0.5948	0.5987	0.6026	0.6064	0.6103	0.6141
0.3	0.6179	0.6217	0.6255	0.6293	0.6331	0.6368	0.6406	0.6443	0.6480	0.6517
0.4	0.6554	0.6591	0.6628	0.6664	0.6700	0.6736	0.6772	0.6808	0.6844	0.6879
0.5	0.6915	0.6950	0.6985	0.7019	0.7054	0.7088	0.7123	0.7157	0.7190	0.7224
0.6	0.7257	0.7291	0.7324	0.7357	0.7389	0.7422	0.7454	0.7486	0.7517	0.7549
0.7	0.7580	0.7611	0.7642	0.7673	0.7704	0.7734	0.7764	0.7794	0.7823	0.7852
0.8	0.7881	0.7910	0.7939	0.7967	0.7995	0.8023	0.8051	0.8078	0.8106	0.8133
0.9	0.8159	0.8186	0.8212	0.8238	0.8264	0.8289	0.8315	0.8340	0.8365	0.8389
1.0	0.8413	0.8438	0.8461	0.8485	0.8508	0.8531	0.8554	0.8577	0.8599	0.8621
1.1	0.8643	0.8665	0.8686	0.8708	0.8729	0.8749	0.8770	0.8790	0.8810	0.8830
1.2	0.8849	0.8869	0.8888	0.8907	0.8925	0.8944	0.8962	0.8980	0.8997	0.9015
1.3	0.9032	0.9049	0.9066	0.9082	0.9099	0.9115	0.9131	0.9147	0.9162	0.9177
1.4	0.9192	0.9207	0.9222	0.9236	0.9251	0.9265	0.9279	0.9292	0.9306	0.9319
1.5	0.9332	0.9345	0.9357	0.9370	0.9382	0.9394	0.9406	0.9418	0.9429	0.9441
1.6	0.9452	0.9463	0.9474	0.9484	0.9495	0.9505	0.9515	0.9525	0.9535	0.9545
1.7	0.9554	0.9564	0.9573	0.9582	0.9591	0.9599	0.9608	0.9616	0.9625	0.9633
1.8	0.9641	0.9649	0.9656	0.9664	0.9671	0.9678	0.9686	0.9693	0.9699	0.9706
1.9	0.9713	0.9719	0.9726	0.9732	0.9738	0.9744	0.9750	0.9756	0.9761	0.9767
2.0	0.9772	0.9778	0.9783	0.9788	0.9793	0.9798	0.9803	0.9808	0.9812	0.9817
2.1	0.9821	0.9826	0.9830	0.9834	0.9838	0.9842	0.9846	0.9850	0.9854	0.9857
2.2	0.9861	0.9864	0.9868	0.9871	0.9875	0.9878	0.9881	0.9884	0.9887	0.9890
2.3	0.9893	0.9896	0.9898	0.9901	0.9904	0.9906	0.9909	0.9911	0.9913	0.9916
2.4	0.9918	0.9920	0.9922	0.9925	0.9927	0.9929	0.9931	0.9932	0.9934	0.9936
2.5	0.9938	0.9940	0.9941	0.9943	0.9945	0.9946	0.9948	0.9949	0.9951	0.9952
2.6	0.9953	0.9955	0.9956	0.9957	0.9959	0.9960	0.9961	0.9962	0.9963	0.9964
2.7	0.9965	0.9966	0.9967	0.9968	0.9969	0.9970	0.9971	0.9972	0.9973	0.9974
2.8	0.9974	0.9975	0.9976	0.9977	0.9977	0.9978	0.9979	0.9979	0.9980	0.9981
2.9	0.9981	0.9982	0.9982	0.9983	0.9984	0.9984	0.9985	0.9985	0.9986	0.9986
3.0	0.9987	0.9987	0.9987	0.9988	0.9988	0.9989	0.9989	0.9989	0.9990	0.9990
3.1	0.9990	0.9991	0.9991	0.9991	0.9992	0.9992	0.9992	0.9992	0.9993	0.9993
3.2	0.9993	0.9993	0.9994	0.9994	0.9994	0.9994	0.9994	0.9995	0.9995	0.9995
3.3	0.9995	0.9995	0.9995	0.9996	0.9996	0.9996	0.9996	0.9996	0.9996	0.9997
3.4	0.9997	0.9997	0.9997	0.9997	0.9997	0.9997	0.9997	0.9997	0.9997	0.9998
3.5	0.9998	0.9998	0.9998	0.9998	0.9998	0.9998	0.9998	0.9998	0.9998	0.9998
3.6	0.9998	0.9998	0.9999	0.9999	0.9999	0.9999	0.9999	0.9999	0.9999	0.9999
3.7	0.9999	0.9999	0.9999	0.9999	0.9999	0.9999	0.9999	0.9999	0.9999	0.9999
3.8	0.9999	0.9999	0.9999	0.9999	0.9999	0.9999	0.9999	0.9999	0.9999	0.9999
3.9	1.0000	1.0000	1.0000	1.0000	1.0000	1.0000	1.0000	1.0000	1.0000	1.0000

6

Sampling Distributions

This chapter is a turning point. This is where we move from simply describing data to using data to make inferences about things we do not know. It is the beginning of inferential statistics. After all, "it's not the figures themselves, it's what you do with them that matters" (K.A.C. Manderville).[1] Every semester, I try to convince my students that statistics is as interesting as the problems it is used to solve. I have taught statistics long enough to know that very few people enjoy the act of crunching numbers in a dataset. Admittedly, you would have to be pretty unique to like that. However, everyone is interested in something, and to answer interesting questions about any topic, we almost always turn to data.

The goal of inferential statistics is to use sample data to estimate unknown characteristics of a larger population. When polling agencies release early estimates for an upcoming election, they are relying on inferential statistics. Biochemists use inferential statistics to develop vaccines to prevent diseases. When businesses decide which marketing platforms to invest in, they use inferential statistics. In fact, most important data-driven decisions rely on statistical inference. In order to use sample data to gain insights into the larger population, we first must understand sampling distributions.

6.1 Defining a Sampling Distribution

Recall from Chapter 3 on descriptive statistics that a distribution of data is simply an organized dataset. Imagine a column of data which contains peoples' annual income, sorted from the smallest to the largest. That column is a distribution of data. In order to better visualize the data, suppose you take that column of income values and construct a histogram. With this histogram in mind, recall that a distribution of data has three important characteristics: (1) its shape, (2) its mean, and (3) its standard deviation.

---

[1] This quote is from a passage of a book titled *The Undoing of Lamia Gurdleneck* by K.A.C. Manderville referenced in *The Advanced Theory of Statistics* by Maurice Kendall and Alan Stuart in 1979. However, neither Manderville nor his book actually exists.

A Guide to Business Statistics, First Edition. David M. McEvoy.
© 2018 John Wiley & Sons, Inc. Published 2018 by John Wiley & Sons, Inc.

A sampling distribution is a particular type of dataset created by drawing different samples of the same size from a given population. Each time a new sample is drawn, a statistic (e.g., mean and proportion) is calculated and added to the dataset. A complete sampling distribution contains statistics from all possible samples of the same size taken from a single population. If the population is finite (i.e., a fixed number of values), then the number of unique samples of a given size is also finite. When a population is infinite, then the number of unique samples is infinite and so is the sampling distribution. As long as population sizes are very large and sample sizes are relatively small, we can treat finite and infinite populations equivalently. We will discuss what is meant by "large" and "small" later in this chapter.

To illustrate the concept of a sampling distribution, suppose the population of interest is a large statistics class of 100 students. Let us say we take a random sample of 10 students from this population and calculate the average grade point average (GPA). What we just calculated is a statistic, and that statistic is random because it comes from a random sample. If we drew another random sample of 10 students, we would likely get a different average GPA value. If everyone in the class were identical, different samples would lead to the same average GPA. Of course, this is not the case. The population is made up of all kinds of students, from bookworms to slackers. And each has the same chance of being in the sample of 10. When we say a unique sample, we mean a collection of 10 students that will not all be together in another sample. So, a single student, call him Johnny Crabcakes, can be part of many unique samples, but never with the same nine people more than once.

The point is that different samples of the same size will lead to different average GPAs, and so the results can vary. A sampling distribution in this example is what we call the entire collection of average GPA values from sample sizes of 10 students. How many unique samples of 10 students can we take from the population of 100 students? To answer this, we rely on the combination formula that is included in the Technical Appendix (Formula A.1). Using the formula, we find that there are 17.3 trillion unique samples of 10 students that can be drawn from a population of 100. That is quite a few.

Now, if we take that sampling distribution (consisting of 17.3 trillion average GPAs) and construct a histogram, it will have its own shape, mean, and standard deviation. We will discuss these characteristics in general, why they are important and how they relate to the underlying population distribution in the sections that follow.

6.2 The Importance of Sampling Distributions

Whenever sample data are used to estimate something that we do not know about a larger population, many different samples of the same size are possible.

From our example with a finite population of 100 students, we found 17.3 trillion unique samples of 10 students. When we consider much larger populations, the number of unique samples can be so numerous that it is effectively impossible to calculate. At least not with Excel or other standard programs. And when the population of interest is infinite (e.g., the production of bottles of coca-cola), then the number of samples is infinite.

While trillions or even an infinite number of samples might be possible, very often statisticians deal with only a single sample. This is because sampling is often expensive and time consuming. They draw one sample from the population and calculate a statistic (e.g., the sample mean). Then, that single sample value is used as the estimate of the unknown population value. The statistician, of course, recognizes that the sample value is only an estimate and it likely differs from the true value. The difference between sample statistics and the population parameters they estimate is called *sampling error*. With this in mind, the statistician would like to know how close the sample statistic is to the true value.

For example, the Internal Revenue Service (IRS) may want to find out, on average, by how much do Americans underreport their income on tax returns. To do so, suppose they audit a random sample of taxpayers. They cannot audit everyone because it would take too long and is extremely costly. Let us say they audit 10,000 Americans as their one sample. The sample of audits is then used to infer the average underreporting for all American taxpayers. Of course, they know that their estimate is not exact because it is drawn from a sample, not the entire population. Their next step is to determine how far their estimate could vary from the true value, and to answer that question they need to know how much sample mean values can vary given the sample size. In other words, they need to know the standard deviation of the distribution of sample means.

To move forward, we need to understand the characteristics (shape, mean, and standard deviation) of the sampling distribution. Let us start with an example.

6.3   An Example of a Sampling Distribution

We will start with a population dataset that is relatively small, so that we can easily construct a complete sampling distribution. Suppose the population of interest is daily commuting times (in minutes) for six workers at a small start-up firm.

The commuting times for the six workers are found in Table 6.1. The frequency histogram in Figure 6.1 plots commuting time for the six workers and shows the shape of the population distribution. The horizontal axis displays the commute time and the frequency is plotted on the vertical axis. The vertical axis could easily be converted into a relative frequency simply by dividing

Table 6.1 Commute time for a population of six workers.

Worker	Commute time (in minutes)
Tim	3
Dave	9
Joe	6
Dennis	15
John	18
Kris	3

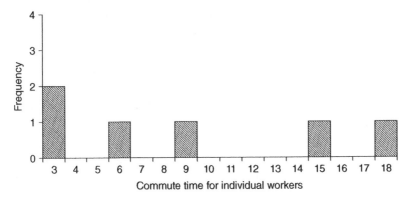

Figure 6.1 Population distribution of commute times.

the frequency in each bin by the total number of workers. The shape of the relative frequency distribution, of course, would be identical to that in Figure 6.1.

From this population dataset, we want to form a sampling distribution. The sampling distribution is created by taking samples from this population of six people. For each sample we draw from this population, we are going to calculate the sample mean. Therefore, the specific sampling distribution we will construct will be the *sampling distribution of a mean*. Note that we can form sampling distributions for any statistic (e.g., the standard deviation or variance), but the mean is a particularly useful one for inference.

Suppose we choose to arbitrarily take samples of size three from the population. How many unique samples of three people can we draw from a population of six people? To answer this question, we again rely on the combination formula and discover that 20 unique samples of size three are possible. These 20 samples are contained in Table 6.2.

For each sample of three above, the sample mean commute times are calculated and provided in Table 6.3. For example, the first cell in the first column of

Table 6.2 All 20 unique samples of size three.

Tim, Dave, Joe	Tim, Joe, John	Dave, Joe, Dennis	Dave, John, Kris
Tim, Dave, Dennis	Tim, Joe, Kris	Dave, Joe, John	Joe, Dennis, John
Tim, Dave, John	Tim, Dennis, John	Dave, Joe, Kris	Joe, Dennis, Kris
Tim, Dave, Kris	Tim, Dennis, Kris	Dave, Dennis, John	Joe, John, Kris
Tim, Joe, Dennis	Tim, John, Kris	Dave, Dennis, Kris	Dennis, John, Kris

Table 6.3 A sampling distribution of the mean.

6	9	10	10
9	4	11	13
10	12	6	8
5	7	14	9
8	8	9	12

Table 6.2 contains workers Tim, Dave, and Joe. Their commute times are three, nine, and six minutes, respectively. So, the average of the sample in the first cell in the first column is $(3 + 6 + 9)/3 = 6$, which appears in the same relative place in Table 6.3.

The dataset in Table 6.3 is the sampling distribution of the mean for a sample size of three people. It contains all possible average commuting times for samples of three workers.

We can visualize the sampling distribution by constructing a frequency histogram. That histogram is included in Figure 6.2 along with the original histogram of the population data above it. When comparing both images, note that the shape of the sampling distribution is dramatically different from the shape of the population it is drawn from. In particular, it is more symmetric and is less spread out. This finding is not unique to our example dataset; it will be true for all data.

We want to make note of one other important comparison in this example. The average commute time of the six workers that make up our population is nine minutes; that is, the mean of the population distribution is nine minutes ($\mu = 9$). *What is the mean of the sampling distribution?* To figure that out, you would have to take the average of all 20 sample averages. Be careful, the language gets tricky here because we are talking about taking a "mean of means." Performing these calculations, we find the average of all 20 sample averages to be also nine minutes. So, the two distributions have the same mean. This relationship will always be the case no matter what dataset you are working with.

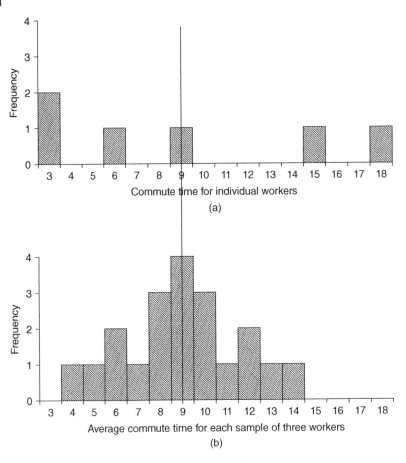

Figure 6.2 Population and sampling distributions of the mean.

Our example with commute times for the six workers is useful to illustrate what a sampling distribution is and how it is formed by sampling from the population. Of course, what we are really interested in is what sampling distributions look like for any kind of population of interest. Whether we are interested in sales data from an advertising campaign, unemployment measures of the national economy, caffeine in a cup of coffee, or the average miles per gallon of a new hybrid vehicle. When we use a sample of data to estimate something we do not know about a population, it would be useful to know what the distribution of all possible samples looks like. It turns out that we are in luck. We now turn to the characteristics of sampling distributions that can be generalized to any situation.

6.4   Characteristics of a Sampling Distribution of a Mean

In our example above, we knew how big the population was, which people made up the population, and what their commute times were. We knew everything we needed to know about the population. In reality, we will not know all of this information about our populations of interest. Remember, the point of inferential statistics is that we are trying to estimate something we are uncertain about. In other words, if you know the relevant information about the whole population, like I did in the example above, there is no need for inferential statistics because there is nothing to infer, you already know the answer you are after. The example was only used to illustrate what a sampling distribution is.

In practice, we will not know a great deal about our populations of interest, so we will not be able to observe complete sampling distributions. Recall, a complete sampling distribution consists of all possible unique samples of a given size from a population. To get all possible unique samples, you would need to have the entire population dataset. For any practical situation, this will not be the case.

Again, think of the IRS trying to determine how much Americans underreport their earnings on their taxes. The IRS knows what the population of interest is; that is, adult Americans and immigrants who are required to pay taxes. They probably do not know exactly how many Americans fall into this population, but they have a ballpark idea. Without auditing, the IRS also does not know the extent of underreporting. They suspect people cheat on their taxes, they suspect it is probably somewhat prevalent, but they do not know for sure. What is really cool about inferential statistics is that all of this uncertainty does not matter. It turns out that even if you do not know much at all about the population you are sampling from, the properties (shape, mean, and standard deviation) of sampling distributions are all predictable.

We will look at these three properties separately. With each property, a definition is presented and then followed by a discussion. We will start with the mean.

6.4.1   The Mean

The average of all possible sample means of a given sample size will equal the population mean.

To be cute, and to hopefully help you remember this property, "the mean of the means is the mean." We already discussed that this was the case from our example of commuting times. The population mean was nine, and so was the average of all 20 sample mean values. This property will always hold.

This property leads to another term that is often used in inferential statistics. Whenever the average of a sample statistic equals the population value, we call that statistic *unbiased*. Something that is biased has a tendency to yield one particular outcome more than others. This is not the case with our sample means. Different samples of the same size will likely yield different results, but they will not be skewed in any one direction. Consider again the IRS taking a sample of audits from its population of taxpayers. If the IRS takes one sample, the average underreporting of income from the sample may be above or below the true mean. The IRS knows this. The IRS also knows that if the sample is random, it is equally likely to get estimates above and below the true value. Therefore, their estimate is not biased from above or below. The notation for this property is found in the Technical Appendix.

6.4.2 The Shape

As long as sample sizes are large enough, the shape of the sampling distribution of the mean will be bell-shaped (i.e., normally distributed).

When we discuss the shape of a distribution of data, it is best to visualize it as a histogram, like the ones from our example in the previous section. Recall that with any interesting case in inferential statistics, we will not have the entire population of data and so we will not know exactly how a histogram of the population data would look. What is amazing, and probably the most important aspect of inferential statistics, is that we do not need to know the shape of the population data. Whether the population is skewed-right, skewed-left, uniform, bell-shaped, bimodal, or just completely crazy, it does not matter. The distribution of sample averages pulled from that population will be bell-shaped.

That sampling distributions will be bell-shaped is a result of one of the most famous theorems in probability theory: the *Central Limit Theorem*. The Central Limit Theorem is fundamental to our understanding and practice of inferential statistics. By the Central Limit Theorem, as long as sample sizes of continuous data are large enough, sampling distributions of the mean will always be normally distributed. What defines a large sample? The rule of thumb is a sample size of 30 or more.

There is an often neglected caveat to the Central Limit Theorem. The theorem holds under the premise that samples are drawn from an infinite population or from a finite population with replacement. Sampling with replacement ensures that the probability of selecting a certain value from the population is not dependent on what values were chosen previously. Note that almost all survey data are gathered by sampling *without* replacement. In other words, with most studies once a person is surveyed, the probability of that person being surveyed again is zero. The good news is that if the population is big enough and the fraction of the population that is sampled is small enough, then we can treat finite populations as if they are infinite and avoid any concern about the with or without replacement issue. The standard rule is that if the sample size is 5% of the population or less, then the population can be treated as if it were infinite (of course, sample sizes need to be at least 30). If the sample is greater than 5% of the population, then a simple correction factor for some of the statistics is needed. We will get to this correction factor when discussing the standard deviation of the sampling distribution.[2]

To illustrate the Central Limit Theorem, consider again the IRS investigating tax fraud. The IRS does not know what the population of data is shaped like because it does not have information on underreporting from all taxpayers. It could be the case that people tend to underreport by the same amount. In this case, the population dataset would follow a uniform distribution. Alternatively, it could be the case that a lot of people underreport by small amounts and only a few people underreport by massive amounts. In this case, the population dataset would likely be right-skewed because you will have extreme underreporting in the right tail of the distribution. The important point is that it does not matter what the shape of the underlying population data is. As long as the IRS audits 30 or more people as its sample, it can be assured that the sample mean they calculate comes from a normally distributed dataset.

In a world of chaos and uncertainty, we can take comfort in knowing that our sampling distributions will always be normal if our sample sizes are large enough. Moreover, a sample size of 30 is not very big at all, so it is typically a low bar to cross. Why is all this so important? When we turn to applications of inferential statistics in the chapters that follow, our analysis will be based on sampling distributions, not the populations they are drawn from. Knowing that those distributions are normal will prove very useful indeed. We already know a great deal about the properties of normally distributed data and we will utilize that information starting with confidence intervals in Chapter 7.

So what about smaller samples, the ones that are less than 30 observations? Can we predict the shape of sampling distributions of the mean for these? The answer is yes, but only in the limited cases in which we know, or are fairly sure, the population is bell shaped. A common example is data on human height. If you created a histogram using height data from any population of interest, you could expect it to be bell shaped. In these cases, when the population is bell

---

2 Another related caveat is that when sampling without replacement from a finite population, it is not always the case that the sampling distribution approaches normality as the sample size increases. In fact, it has been shown that the shape of the sampling distribution of a mean for a sample of size n is identical to the shape of the sampling distribution of the mean for a sample of size $N - n$ (see Plane, D.R., and K.R. Gordon (1982)) "A simple proof of the nonapplicability of the Central Limit Theorem to finite populations." The American Statistician 36(3): 175–176). Suppose that our population is of size 100 and our sample is of size 95. In this case, there is no reason to assume that the sampling distribution for $n = 95$ would approach the normal distribution. The intuition for this property can be drawn from the combination formula. The number of unique samples for $n = 95$ from $N = 100$ is the same as the number of unique samples of $n = 5$ from $N = 100$. Since a sample size of five is too small to assume that the sampling distribution is normal, so too is a sample size of 95 given this finite population.

shaped, then the sampling distribution of the mean will be bell shaped for any sample size.

For all other cases with sample sizes less than 30, the ones in which we do not have a good feel for the shape of the population, or the ones in which we know the population is not normal, we cannot predict the shape of the sampling distribution with such small samples. Note that our previous example of commuting times falls into this category. The population is clearly not bell-shaped (Figure 6.1). The sampling distribution is certainly symmetric and is closer to being bell-shaped compared to the population (Figure 6.2), but it is not quite there. The reason is that the sample size is only three. The sample size is too small to rely on the Central Limit Theorem and its shape is not quite normal. The take-away message for this property is that if we are taking a sample of continuous data, we should always strive for sizes greater than 30 to eliminate uncertainty as to what shape the sampling distribution will take on.

6.4.3 The Standard Deviation

The standard deviation of the sampling distribution is always smaller than the standard deviation of the population, and it gets even smaller with bigger sample sizes.

From Figure 6.2, you may notice that the sampling distribution (histogram on the bottom) is less spread out compared to the population (histogram on the top). This relationship will always be true. Recall from Chapter 3 that a standard deviation is an average deviation from a mean. It is our chosen measure of how variable, or spread-out datasets are. The distribution of sample means also has a standard deviation. To distinguish between populations and sampling distributions, we call the standard deviation of the sampling distribution the *standard error*.

As the size of the sample increases, the sample means become less spread out. To use the new jargon, as our sample sizes increase, the standard error decreases. The reason is because with bigger samples the more extreme values in the population become diluted with the more central values. Let us use income data for adult Americans as an example. Even without having population data at our disposal, we know that there is a large amount of variability in incomes. Driving much of that variability is the small fraction of very wealthy Americans. Figure 6.3 is a stylized graph (not produced with real data) of income values. Rather than a histogram, for convenience, we use a smooth line to depict the shape of the population data. Notice that the dataset is dramatically right-skewed. The population data are very spread out mainly because of the extreme income values (Richie Rich and the 1% on the graph). The incomes of Richie Rich and the 1% are dramatically far from the population mean income levels, and those deviations factor into the calculation of the population standard deviation. This is why income data, even if we cannot directly observe all of them, have a large standard deviation.

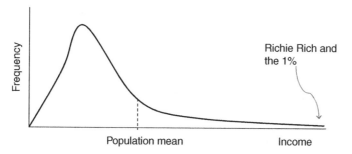

Figure 6.3 Population income data of adult Americans.

Now, if we were to take a sample from this population (say a sample consisting of 100 people), and calculate their average income, it is possible that we get Richie Rich or another 1% member as part of our sample. But, that extreme income value (or values) will be watered down with more central income values on the left side of the distribution. It is for this reason that the average income values (taken from samples) will vary less than individual income values (from the population). And the bigger the sample size, the more watered down the extreme values become. Another way to look at it is this: the closer our sample size is to the population size, the closer our sample means will be to the population mean.

When the sampling distribution can be assumed to be normal, the standard error is calculated by taking the standard deviation of the population and dividing it by the square root of the sample size (i.e., $\sigma/\sqrt{n}$). See Formula A.3.

In the previous section, we mentioned that if the sample we take is greater than 5% of a finite population, then we have to slightly adjust our approach. In particular, our calculation of the standard error is made with what is called the *finite population correction factor*. The correction is simply multiplying $\sqrt{\frac{N-n}{N-1}}$ by the standard error (see Formula A.4). Since $N - n$ is always smaller than $N - 1$, the correction factor is less than one. Therefore, the correction reduces the standard error of the sampling distribution as the fraction of the population that is sampled increases. The intuition is that as the sample size approaches the population size, we have a more precise measure of the level of variation in the data. In reality, the correction factor can be applied to all samples drawn from finite populations, however it becomes irrelevant (i.e., effectively equals one) for samples less than 5% of the population and so it is dropped from the analysis.

6.4.4 Finding Probabilities With a Sampling Distribution

To illustrate the relationship between a population distribution and a sampling distribution of a mean, we can look at an example. Again, consider a large register of grades from a course in business statistics (over 1000 students).

The grade distribution of the population, like most grade distributions, is left-skewed because most students score in the 60–100 range while only a small fraction totally bomb which brings down the average. The population mean is 80 and the population standard deviation – the average deviation around the mean – is 6 points.

Now, consider a sampling distribution of the mean for samples of size 36. Again, the sampling distribution is the average grades for all unique samples of 36 students. We have enough information to know that (1) the mean of the sampling distribution will equal the population mean of 80, (2) the distribution will be normal by the Central Limit Theorem because the sample size exceeds 30, and (3) the standard deviation of the sampling distribution – called the standard error – is $6/\sqrt{36} = 1$ point.[3] Both the population distribution and the sampling distribution are illustrated in Figure 6.4.

The graph on top of Figure 6.4 is the population distribution of course grades. Note the label x on the horizontal axis and that the shape is left-skewed. The graph below is the sampling distribution of the mean. Take note that the mean equals the population mean, the shape is normal and that the standard error (i.e., the standard deviation of the sample means) is 1 point. A comparison of the graphs reveals that the variation in the population grades is much greater

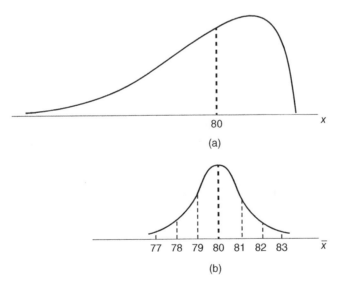

Figure 6.4 Population distribution and sampling distribution ($n = 36$) of course grades in statistics.

3 Note also that since our sample of 36 is only 3.6% of a finite population of size 1000, we do not need to use a finite population correction factor when calculating the standard error.

than the variation in the sample mean grades. We can use these properties of the sampling distribution to find the probabilities of specific events.

Question: What is the probability that the average grade from a sample of 36 students is less than 83?

To answer this question, we can again rely on our knowledge of the normal distribution. A grade of 83 is clearly three standard errors above the mean of 80. In other words, the z-score $= (83 - 80)/1 = 3$. The Empirical Rule tells us that just about all of the data will fall within three standard errors of the mean. To be more precise, we can consult the z-table. Looking up $z = 3.0$ yields a probability of 0.9987, which is the probability of getting an average grade less than 83 from a random sample of 36 students. To flip the question on its head, there is only a 0.0013 chance of the sample average being 83 or greater.

6.5 Sampling Distribution of a Proportion

When data are categorical in nature, the proportion, not the mean, is often the measure of interest. The proportion is simply the number of observations that take on a certain category divided by the total number of observations. If a population of $N = 1000$ students consists of 555 females, then the *population proportion* of females is $555/1000 = 0.55$. We denote the population proportion with the Greek letter $\pi = 0.55$ (π is the same notation we used for the probability of a success in Chapter 5). When a proportion is calculated from a sample of data (taken from a larger population) that statistic is denoted as p. For example, if a sample of size $n = 100$ is taken and 60 out of the 100 students are females, the *sample proportion* is $p = 0.60$.

Just like for the sampling distribution of the mean, we would like to know how the distribution of all sample proportions for a given sample size looks like. That is, what is the shape, the mean, and the standard deviation? We need this information because, often, we use sample proportions to estimate an unknown value of a population proportion. Meaning, we use p as an estimate of π when we cannot get our hands on the entire population of data.

However, to understand the idea of a sampling distribution of a proportion p, we start in a simplified word in which we have the population data. Again, consider our example in which the population of interest is 1000 students and 555 of them are female, so that $\pi = 0.55$. Again, also consider a random sample of $n = 100$ students taken from that population. We should not expect our random sample to yield a proportion exactly equal to the population proportion. Why? Because we are getting only a partial picture of the true value. Just a taste. If one sample of 100 yields a sample proportion of 0.60 females (600 of 1000), another random sample of 100 could easily result in a sample proportion of 0.50 females (500 of 1000). This is again the idea of sampling error, which is the difference between sample statistics and population parameter values. The point is that the statistic p is a random variable because it is derived from a random sample. That said, under certain conditions, we can be confident what the characteristics (the shape, mean, and standard deviation) of the sampling distribution will be.

6.5.1   The Mean

It turns out that if we took all possible unique samples of a given size n, and for each calculated the sample proportion p, the average of all those sample proportions would equal the population proportion. Therefore, on average, the sample proportion will equal the population proportion. This means that the sample proportion p is an unbiased estimate of the population proportion π. The importance of this result is that even if we did not know the value of π (which will be the case in all real-world applications of inferential statistics), we know that the collection of all possible sample proportions will be distributed evenly around it. This property will hold for any sample size.

6.5.2   The Shape

Like the sampling distribution of the mean, the shape of the sampling distribution of a proportion depends on the sample size. What is cool (if statistics can be cool) is that if the sample size is large enough, then the sampling distribution can be approximated as normal. How large does the sample need to be? As long as $n \times \pi \geq 10$ and $n \times (1 - \pi) \geq 10$, then we can assume that the shape of the sampling distribution is normal. When these two conditions are satisfied, we call that the *normal approximation of the binomial distribution*. In those cases, the distribution will follow a z-distribution, which means that we already have a good understanding of what it looks like and how to calculate the probabilities.

You may be asking yourself in the real-world situations in which we do not know the value of π, how can we determine if our sampling distribution can be approximated as normal? Well, in those cases, we simply plug in our sample proportion. This would be $n \times p \geq 10$ and $n \times (1 - p) \geq 10$.

6.5.3   The Standard Deviation

We call the standard deviation of a sampling distribution the standard error. It measures the average deviation of p from π for a given sample size (see formula A.7). The intuition is that as the sample size goes up, the closer the sample proportion is going to be clustered around the population proportion. Therefore, as the sample size goes up, the *standard error of a proportion* goes down.

Let us take a look at a few graphs in order to get a better feel for the relationship between n and the sampling distribution of a proportion. We will continue with the example of a population of size $N = 1000$ and a population proportion of $\pi = 0.55$. We will consider three sampling distributions, one where $n = 5$, one where $n = 25$, and one where $n = 100$. In each case, the graph in Figure 6.5 shows the relative frequencies of values for p for all possible samples of size n. The axes are removed to better highlight two points regarding the relative shapes. (1) As the sample size goes up, the sampling distribution of a proportion is closer to normal in shape and (2) as the sample size goes up, there is less variability in sample proportions.[4]

The usefulness of knowing these characteristics can easily be applied to polling results we see in our everyday life. Take again the presidential approval rating. To arrive at those ratings about 1000 people are randomly sampled and asked whether or not they approve of how the current president is handling his responsibilities. The dataset would have a "1" marked for each person that

Figure 6.5 Sampling distributions for proportions when $\pi = 0.55$ at different sample sizes.

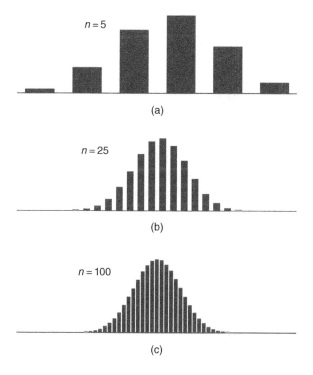

---

4 As with the sampling distribution for the mean, if samples are drawn from a finite population without replacement and the sample size exceeds 5% of the population, then the standard error is calculated using a correction factor (see Formula A.8). When samples are drawn without replacement from a finite population, the distribution technically follows a *hypergeometric distribution* rather than a binomial distribution. However, as long as sample sizes are small relative to the population size, the sampling distribution can be approximated using a binomial distribution, which is the approach taken in this text as with many others.

approves and a "0" for all others. One sample is taken in a given time period and a sample statistic is reported. Let us say 480 people indicated approval, so the sample proportion is 480/1000 = 0.48. Of course, the approval rating for all Americans may be different from 0.48, but we know that the sampling distribution for samples of size 1000 can be approximated as normal, and will be centered around the true value. This information is going to be used directly in our analysis of confidence intervals (Chapter 7) and hypothesis testing (Chapters 8 and 9).

6.6 Summary

Inferential statistics is all about using sample data to shed light on something we do not know about a population. The chapters that follow on confidence intervals, hypothesis testing, and regression analysis are all tools of inference, and they all require taking samples from a population. If sampling is done randomly, then different samples can lead to different results. This chapter on sampling distributions was all about describing what the distribution of different sample results will look like.

Let us reiterate the three properties of a sampling distribution of the mean for continuous data. (1) The mean of the sampling distribution equals the population mean. (2) By the Central Limit Theorem, if sample sizes are 30 or more, then the shape of the sampling distribution is normal. For sample sizes smaller than 30, the sampling distribution will be normal only if the population is known to be normal. (3) The standard deviation of the sampling distribution – called the standard error – decreases in the sample size and is strictly less than the population standard deviation (formula given in A.3).

Finally, the three properties of a sampling distribution of a proportion are: (1) The mean of the sampling distribution equals the population proportion, (2) if the sample size is large enough, then the distribution of sample proportions can be approximated as normal, and (3) the standard deviation of the sampling distribution – called the standard error – decreases in the sample size (formula given in A.7).

Technical Appendix

To find out how many unique samples can be drawn from a fixed population, we use the *combination formula*:

$$C_n^N = \frac{N!}{n!(N-n)!},$$ (A.1)

where C stands for combinations, N is the population size (e.g., the number of people in the population of interest), and n is the sample size. The symbol ! is the factorial symbol. For example, $4! = 4 \times 3 \times 2 \times 1$.

Recall, the mean of a population for variable x is typically denoted as μ_x (most often the x subscript is dropped for convenience). The mean of the sampling distribution – the mean of all sample means – is denoted as $\mu_{\bar{x}}$. Note the difference in the subscript. It will always be the case that the mean of the sampling distribution is equal to the mean of the population:

$$\mu_{\bar{x}} = \mu_x.$$ (A.2)

When the sampling distribution can be approximated as normal its standard deviation – the standard error – is equal to the population standard deviation divided by the square root of the sample size. The *standard error of a mean* is

$$\sigma_{\bar{x}} = \frac{\sigma_x}{\sqrt{n}},$$ (A.3)

where σ_x is the population standard deviation. Note that the standard error goes down as n goes up. In cases in which samples are drawn from a finite population without replacement and the sample size is greater than 5% of the population, then the standard error is calculated using a *finite population correction factor*. In this case, the standard error is

$$\sigma_{\bar{x}} = \frac{\sigma_x}{\sqrt{n}} \sqrt{\frac{N-n}{N-1}},$$ (A.4)

and will be strictly less than the standard error calculated without the correction. The z-score for a sampling distribution of a mean is:

$$z = \frac{\bar{x} - \mu_{\bar{x}}}{\sigma_{\bar{x}}}.$$ (A.5)

The sampling distribution of a proportion can be *approximated as normal* if:

$$n\pi \geq 10$$
$$n(1-\pi) \geq 10.$$ (A.6)

The *standard error of a proportion* is

$$\sigma_p = \sqrt{\frac{\pi(1-\pi)}{n}},$$ (A.7)

In cases in which samples are drawn from a finite population without replacement and the sample size is greater than 5% of the population, then the standard error is calculated using a *finite population correction factor*. In this case, the standard error is

$$\sigma_p = \sqrt{\frac{\pi(1-\pi)}{n}}\sqrt{\frac{N-n}{N-1}}, \qquad (A.8)$$

and will be strictly less than the standard error calculated without the correction. The z-score for a sampling distribution of a proportion is:

$$z = \frac{p - \pi}{\sigma_p}. \qquad (A.9)$$

7

Confidence Intervals

In the days leading up to the 2012 presidential election, my brother called me fired up about some recent polling results. The polling agency reported that the percentage of Americans who were planning to vote for Barack Obama on November 6 – election day – was 49%. Roughly 200 million Americans were registered to vote in the last election and the poll results were based on – wait for it – 1300 people.[1] My brother quickly dismissed the results, arguing that there is no way a sample of 1300 could accurately reflect the preferences of a population of 200 million voters. "I mean, that's a tiny fraction of Americans that was sampled, so it must be bogus." He is right, but only about the sample size being small. The sample is roughly 0.00065% of the population of interest. That *is* a small sample relative to the population size. I was not part of that sample, and if I were a betting man, I would wager that you were not either. But, here is the thing, he was probably wrong about the results being bogus. In fact, not only was a sample size of 1300 adequate for the election polling, it was deliberately chosen as the target sample size.

Let us be clear though. The actual number of registered voters who planned on voting for Obama was probably not exactly 49% like the report found. The chance of that happening – a sample value equaling the true value – is extremely low. It is effectively zero. The polling agency, of course, understands this and that is why they report another statistic along with their main headline result. That statistic is called the *margin of error*, and it is the fundamental building block of what we call *confidence intervals*. The problem is that often the margin of error in popular polls is demoted to a footnote or relegated to a supplementary section housed on another website. The margin of error, in other words, often gets second shrift. This is a shame, because the margin of error contains all

---

1 Note that the population of interest for those conducting election polls is "likely voters" that is less than the number of registered voters.

A Guide to Business Statistics, First Edition. David M. McEvoy.
© 2018 John Wiley & Sons, Inc. Published 2018 by John Wiley & Sons, Inc.

of the information required to actually make sense of the polling agency's result. The margin of error defines the range of values (called an interval) in which the polling agency is confident the true value lies. This is the polling agency's confidence interval. As long as the sample size is less than the population size, then this interval always exists. Make no mistake, when a polling agency publishes a headline like 49% of likely voters are planning on voting for Barack Obama on the election day, they do not mean exactly that. What they really mean is that they are very confident that the percentage of Americans planning on voting for Obama is between, for example, 46 and 52%.

The rest of this chapter walks through what the margin of error is, its role in forming the confidence interval, and how the confidence interval can be correctly interpreted. We will cover the margin of error and confidence intervals for both sample means and sample proportions. The concepts in this chapter rely heavily on the material from Chapter 6 on sampling distributions. So, if you were looking for an excuse to dive back into Chapter 6, then this is it. You know you want to.

7.1 Confidence Intervals for Means

Derek Hamburger is a freshman at a large 4-year university. His friends, who are clearly a clever bunch, call him "Burger." Burger has not yet declared a major and is weighing his options. He is considering a number of majors, and economics is one of them (obviously, Burger is crazy). One of the most important pieces of information Burger is using to make his decision is the average starting salary. You see, Burger, like many of his peers, wants to make sure that he can make a decent living in the career he pursues. In a perfect world, Burger could look into the future, determine what his desired job will be, plan on securing that job, and know exactly what it will pay. Of course, this is not how it works. There is a great deal of uncertainty in Burger's future. One thing he can do, however, is find out on average how much money recent graduates from his institution are earning. This information will at least give him a feel for what he could expect to earn. He could use that information to *infer* what he will earn after graduation.

So, Derek Hamburger visits the placement office in the business school. The office keeps record of recent graduates' starting salaries, but the dataset is incomplete. The data are gathered by surveying recent graduates and rely on voluntary responses. For the most recent graduating classes, there are 75 responses out of a possible 1600 graduates. That is, a sample of data is available, not the population dataset. With this information, Derek cannot know exactly how much the most recent graduating students earned as their starting salary. However, he can make some informed inferences about starting salaries using the sample data.

What Burger does next is load the dataset of 75 responses into a software program like Microsoft Excel.[2] He quickly computes the sample average and sample standard deviation (see Formulas A.2 and A.7 in Chapter 3). He discovers a mean salary of $45,000 and a standard deviation of $5000. He also observes that the data are right-skewed because a handful of former students landed in pretty high-paying jobs. For example, Mikey Moneybags (from a long line of Moneybags) reported a starting salary of $100,000. On the other hand, the lowest earner, Sally Smallchange earned $25,000. So, there is variation in salaries, and they are not distributed symmetrically.

Most importantly, Derek is smart enough to recognize that the actual average of the 1600 graduates is likely different from $45,000 because the sample size is less than the population. But how different? Let us help Derek make sense of his data.

7.1.1 The Characteristics of the Sampling Distribution

Derek is in possession of one unique sample of 75 starting salaries. How many unique samples of 75 are possible out of a population of 1600? Again, relying on the combination formula (Formula A.1 from Chapter 6), there are 1.41×10^{130} possible samples. That is an incredible amount (remove the decimal point and add 128 zeros after 141). But, even with just our single sample, we have a pretty detailed idea of what the distribution of all possible sample means looks like. First, because of the Central Limit Theorem, we know that the collection of all possible sample means can be approximated as normal (sample size $\geq$ 30). And the mean of all possible sample means is the population mean (whatever that number may be).

The collection of sample means calculated from all possible samples of 75 has its own standard deviation. Recall from Chapter 6, we call this the standard error of the mean. The standard error is the population standard deviation divided by the square root of the sample size. The important point is that there is less variation in the sample means than the variation in the population salary data.

Unfortunately, Burger does not know what the standard deviation is for the entire population. He only has a sample standard deviation of $5000, which is the best information he has regarding the unknown value. He will use this value to *estimate* the standard error of the sampling distribution. He simply takes the $5000 and divides by the square root of the sample size of 75. The estimate of the standard error is $5,000/\sqrt{75} = \$577.35$.

When an estimate of the standard error is used in place of a population value, there is more uncertainty about the shape of the distribution. If sample sizes are

---

2 The analysis assumes that the sample of 75 observations is a random sample. If the sample in reality is a nonrandom convenience sample, then it will likely introduce biases (e.g., nonresponse bias), as it will overrepresent students who are willing to provide salary information.

large enough, it is usually still permissible to assume that it is approximately normal and the Empirical Rule and z-table can be utilized. However, a more conservative approach is to assume that it follows what is called a *t-distribution* (or the Student's t-distribution). The t-distribution is symmetric like the z, but a little flatter and less bell-shaped (see Figure 7.2).

We will use the characteristics of the sampling distribution to discuss two approaches to forming confidence intervals around a sample mean. In the first approach, we will assume that the sampling distribution follows a z-distribution. Since we have worked with the Empirical Rule and the z-table in detail in Chapter 5, this approach provides a familiar starting point. Then, we will form a confidence interval assuming that the distribution of sample means follows a t-distribution and highlight the small differences in the results.

7.1.2 Confidence Intervals Using the z-Distribution

Even with all of this information, we still cannot tell Burger exactly what the average starting salary is for all of his former classmates. We never will. But, we can use information from the sampling distribution of the mean to get a pretty good idea. The end goal is to establish a range around the sample mean of $45,000 that we are confident contains the true but unknown value.

The first step toward this goal is choosing the level of confidence. If we wanted to be absolutely 100% confident that our range contained the true value, then all we would have to do is specify ridiculously extreme values. For example, Burger can be 100% confident that the true average starting salary is between zero and one trillion dollars. No one could argue with that. However, this information is not at all informative. It is for this reason that we never specify confidence intervals of 100%. They are not useful. The convention, however, is pretty well established. Confidence intervals are typically calculated at the 99%, 95%, or 90% level of confidence. The most common, by far, is the 95% confidence interval. In fact, if a statistical report includes a confidence interval, but does not specify the level, you can bet it is the 95% confidence level.

Following standard practice, let us choose the 95% confidence level to build the interval for Derek Hamburger. We need to determine the range (lower and upper values) that defines the 95% confidence interval. A useful first step is to think back about the Empirical Rule. If a distribution is normal, then roughly 95% of all the data is within two standard deviations of the mean. For our data that would be two times the standard error amount of $577.35, which is $1154.70. If we were to use this number, then the range would have a lower bound of ($45,000 − $1154.70) and an upper bound of ($45,000 + $1154.70). While the Empirical Rule is useful for a quick approximation, the interval we actually use is a bit more precise.

Instead of using two standard deviations approximated from the Empirical Rule, we are going to use what is called a *critical value*. The critical value is the number of standard errors the upper and lower bounds are away from the sample mean. If the sampling distribution is normal, then the critical value is a z-score found using the cumulative z-table found in the Technical Appendix in Chapter 5. You can also rely on statistical software programs to generate critical values (see Formula A.2). Recall, a z-score tells you how many standard deviations a certain number is away from the mean of any normal distribution. The critical z value for the 95% confidence interval is 1.96. Note that 1.96 is very close to the approximation of 2.0 made by the Empirical Rule. As in the example above, the upper bound to the interval is found by adding 1.96 standard errors to the sample mean. See Formula A.3 for the confidence interval formula using z.

The distance between the sample mean and the upper or lower bound is called the *margin of error*. The margin of error is the critical value × the standard error (Formula A.1). Here, the margin of error is $577.35 × 1.96 = $1131.61. The lower bound is therefore $45,000 minus the margin of error and the upper bound is $45,000 plus the margin of error. The total width of the confidence interval is two times the margin of error. The confidence interval in its entirety is $43,868.39 − $46,131.61.

The interpretation of the interval is the following: Burger is 95% confident that the true average starting salary is between $43,868.39 and $46,131.61.

Question: Why is Derek Burger 95% confident that this interval contains the unknown population mean?

Figure 7.1 illustrates the sampling distribution for the mean. The 95% confidence interval is the width between the two dotted vertical lines. That is the exact size of any interval calculated from a sample of size 75. So, of all possible sample means, the only intervals that would not contain the true mean are the ones that fall in the shaded areas in the tails. Each of those tails contains 2.5% of all means. So, in total, only 5% of all sample means would have intervals around them that would not contain the true mean. The other 95% of

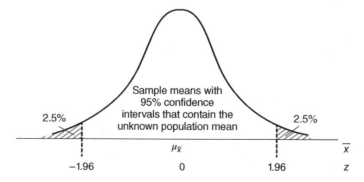

Figure 7.1 95% confidence intervals for the sampling distribution of the mean.

intervals will contain the true unknown value. This is where the interpretation comes from.

Derek Burger should be pretty confident – 95% confident to be exact – that the average starting salary for the last cohort of economics majors was between $43,868.39 and $46,131.61.

Here is a question to think about. How would the interval change if Burger constructed the 99% confidence interval around his sample mean of $4500 instead of the 95% confidence interval? Before even going to the z-table to find the correct critical value and computing the upper and lower bounds, first use your intuition about confidence intervals to answer this. If Burger wants to be more confident that his interval contains the true value, then his interval *must* be wider. Therefore, holding everything else the same, more confidence translates into wider intervals. When the level of confidence is 99% it means that only 1% of all possible confidence intervals for a given sample size will not contain the true population value. Before, with a 95% confidence interval, 5% of all intervals would not contain the true value.

When a level of confidence is chosen, the percentage that remains out of 100% is called the *level of significance*. So, for 99%, 95%, and 90% confidence, the levels of significance are 1%, 5%, and 10%, respectively.

7.1.3   Confidence Intervals Using the *t*-Distribution

While it is often considered acceptable to use a critical z value to construct the confidence interval for a mean, even when the population standard deviation is unknown, there is a more conservative approach. The reason to be more conservative is that we used the sample of 75 to estimate two statistics, the mean and the standard deviation. If for some reason, we knew the value for the population standard deviation, then we could safely rely on the z-distribution. Since we do not know the value for the population standard deviation (which is almost always the case), we must rely on our estimate of $5000. To deal with this added uncertainty about the sampling distribution, we use a more conservative distribution than z. We use what is called the Student t-distribution or simply the t-distribution.

The t-distribution, like the normal distribution, is symmetric and mound-shaped. In fact, when sample sizes are large, the t-distribution and the z-distribution are effectively identical and therefore it does not matter which distribution you use. The t-distribution only becomes influential, and therefore important, with smaller sample sizes. With small sample sizes (0 to 30, for example), the t-distribution looks like a normal distribution that has been stretched out a bit (see Figure 7.2 for a visual comparison). Imagine someone pulling both tails of the distribution slightly. The tails become a bit "fatter" than those in the z-distribution and the bell shape looks flatter. In practical terms, this means that for any given level of confidence, critical

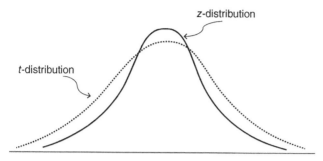

Figure 7.2 A comparison of the z-distribution with the t-distribution when sample sizes are small. When sample sizes get bigger, the t-distribution converges to the z-distribution.

t-values will be bigger than critical z-values when sample sizes are small. And when critical values are bigger, confidence intervals are wider. And a wider interval is a more conservative interval.[3]

Question: When do we use the t-distribution instead of the z-distribution when forming a confidence interval around a mean?

Answer: When we do not know the population standard deviation and the sampling distribution can be approximated as normal.

Now back to Derek Hamburger and his quest to understand the starting salaries of recent economics majors. He wants to take the more conservative approach to calculating the 95% confidence interval for average starting salary. The approach is the same as that used in the previous section with the z-distribution except that the critical value will now be a critical t value (see Formula A.6). Burger will get this value from the t-table. A version of the t-table can be found in the Technical Appendix to this chapter (Table 7.2).

Here is how you use the table. The first column contains what are called degrees of freedom. The formula for degrees of freedom is the sample size minus one. So, Burger's sample has 74 degrees of freedom. The closest row we have to 74 is 70, so that is the value you will use. Next, we have to match the row with 70 degrees of freedom with the appropriate column. To figure out which column, simply calculate what fraction of the sample means fall into each tail of the distribution. With a confidence level of 95%, we know that 2.5% of means will fall into each tail. Therefore, the column we look for has a value of 0.025. The intersection of the row with 70 degrees of freedom and the column of 0.025 yields a critical t-value = 1.994. Note that 1.994 is greater than 1.96 (the z critical value for the 95% confidence levels). Note that you can also use a software program to locate critical t values (see Formula A.5 for the function

---

3 Using the t-distribution for samples with fewer than 30 degrees of freedom comes with an additional caveat. In these cases, it is assumed that the population distribution is normal.

Table 7.1 Comparing 95% confidence intervals using critical z and t values.

	Critical value	Margin of error	Lower limit	Upper limit
z-distribution	1.96	$1131.61	$43,868.39	$46,131.61
t-distribution	1.994	$1151.24	$43,848.76	$46,151.24

in Excel). The margin of error using the t critical value is therefore $577.35 × 1.994 = $1151.24 (Formula A.4). So, as expected, the confidence interval with t is slightly wider than that with z. A comparison of 95% confidence intervals using z and t is made in Table 7.1. As the sample size gets bigger, the differences between z and t get smaller.

7.2 Confidence Intervals for Proportions

Let us get back to the polling results I mentioned at the beginning of this chapter. Recall, the polling agency reported that 49% of 1300 respondents were planning on casting their vote for Barack Obama in the upcoming election back in 2012. The sample statistic of 49% was used to infer what percentage of *all* likely American voters were planning on voting for Obama on the election day. The decision to vote for Obama is binary (yes or no), and therefore the statistic of interest is a proportion (or a percentage if we multiple it by 100) rather than an average. Since the sample size is such a small fraction of a large finite population, the sampling distribution can be assumed to follow a binomial distribution. As introduced in Chapter 6 on sampling distributions, when data are binary and follow a binomial distribution, we treat it a bit differently than continuous data.

The polling agency took one unique sample of 1300 from the population of likely voters. There are hundreds of millions of unique samples that could be drawn from such a large population and the agency only has one. So, it is probably safe to assume that their sample estimate of 49% is different from the true population percentage. For this reason, polling agencies also must provide a margin of error. As with the mean, the margin of error will define the upper and lower bounds to the confidence interval for a proportion. For a 95% confidence level, the agency will be able to say that they are 95% confident that the true percentage of Americans planning on voting for Obama is between an upper and lower bound with 49% in the middle.

To determine the size of the margin of error, we must again rely on our understanding of sampling distributions. In our example, the sampling distribution is the collection of all possible sample proportions from a sample size of 1300. Of course, we will never actually observe this distribution because we only have one sample. However, we know some very important things about it. First, we know that on average the sample proportion will equal the true population proportion. We also know that our sample size is large enough to approximate the sampling distribution as normal (see Formula A.1). Therefore, because it can be assumed normal, we can use the z-distribution to form our confidence interval. Note that, unlike with the mean, we never rely on the t-distribution when forming confidence intervals for proportions.

The margin of error, as with the mean, is calculated as the critical z value × the standard error. The critical z value for the 95% confidence interval is 1.96. The standard error of a binomial distribution is estimated using Formula A.8 and is calculated as 0.0139. Therefore, the margin of error is equal to 1.96 × 0.0139 = 0.027 or 2.7%. With this, we know the size of the 95% confidence interval for the polling agency's report (see equation A.9). That is, the agency was 95% confident that the true percentage of likely voters who were planning on voting for Obama was between 46.3% and 51.7%.

It is important to understand why the polling agency is this confident that their interval contains the true unknown value. The reason is that 95% of all possible intervals created from the sample size of 1300 *will* contain the true value. And only 5% of all possible intervals will not contain it. The interpretation of a confidence interval directly depends on your understanding of sampling distributions. We will find out that understanding sampling distributions is the key to understanding inferential statistics in general, and therefore a key to a happy life.

7.3 Sample Size and the Width of Confidence Intervals

One of the useful things about taking a course in statistics is that you start to view reported data through a more sophisticated lens. Hopefully, you will start to look more deeply into what statistics are being reported in the news, what the population of interest is, how the sample was drawn from the population, what the sample size is, and how large is the margin of error. Statisticians have control of certain elements of their study, while some elements are beyond their control. They can determine their sampling procedure. They can, to some degree, determine the level of confidence they want to report. However, the conventions of 99%, 95%, and 90% are pretty rigid. Most importantly, however, they have control over deciding the size of their sample. The relationship between the width of a confidence interval and the sample size is relatively straightforward. The bigger the margin of error, the wider the interval. The bigger the sample size, the smaller the margin of error. So, holding everything else the same, as the sample size increases the margin of error and the width of the confidence interval decrease. The intervals are tighter with bigger samples.

Consider our example of the percentage of voters who planned on voting for Obama in a previous presidential election. The agency chose a sample size of 1300, such a small fraction of the larger population. You may ask yourself why they did not increase their sample size to try to capture more potential voters. After all, larger samples lead to more precise intervals. The answer is that sampling is costly and so businesses would prefer to minimize their expenditures on sampling given that they meet certain objectives. Those objectives have to do with the margin of error. As you look more carefully at news reports with your developing statistician's eye, you may notice that the margin of error for most studies is 3% or less. A 3% margin of error for the 95% confidence interval has developed into a sort of norm for the maximum allowable margin of error.

Question: What is the smallest sample size required to meet a target of 3% margin of error?

To answer this question, we simply equate the formula for the margin of error to 3% and then solve for the required sample size (see Formula A.11). When doing this, we find that a sample size of 1068 will achieve this target. This should help explain why many polls have sample sizes between 1000 and 1500 participants. These polls meet the 3% margin of error requirement without overspending on sampling.

7.4 Comparing Two Proportions From the Same Poll

On November 9, 2016, many Americans woke up to surprising news. Donald Trump was elected the next president of the United States. Weeks before the election almost all of the national polls had Clinton in the lead. While nobody doubted that Trump had a significant number of supporters, the polling data showed Clinton a clear winner. Or so it seemed.

With political horse races like the Trump–Clinton runoff, people are primarily interested in the difference in support for each candidate. Given the nature of the electoral college in the United States, the interesting polls are those from states that historically have toggled support between political parties, the so-called battleground states. One of the key battleground states is Florida. One cable news network (CNN) poll ($n = 1006$) taken in early November reported that 49% of respondents were planning on voting for Clinton while Trump had 47%. While this was just one poll of many, Clinton had a 1 to 3% point lead in almost all of the polls taken during the same time period.

When the results finally came in, Trump captured 49.1% of the votes to Clinton's 47.8% and he won Florida. Many Americans seemed surprised. Did the polls get it wrong? Probably not.[4]

---

4 Some analysts do question the integrity of the polling results from the 2016 election. There is speculation that some voters may have indicated that they were undecided or they intended to

The margin of error for the 95% confidence interval for each statistic was roughly 3%. Implicitly, the poll reported with 95% confidence that the true percentage of Americans planning on voting for Clinton was between 46 and 52 (and between 44 and 50 for Trump). The actual results from the Florida election clearly fall within those ranges. More important, however, is to consider the estimated difference between the two results from the same poll. The CNN poll had Clinton leading by 2% points. If you follow election coverage, you may have heard pollsters report that two candidates are "within the margin of error" or "outside the margin of error." When a lead is "outside the margin of error," we think of that as a statistically significant lead. A lead not attributed to the sampling error. Here is the important point: the *margin of error for the difference in two proportions* from the same poll is not the same as the margin of error reported in the study (e.g., the 3% in the CNN poll).

It is clear that the confidence intervals for the results for Trump and Clinton overlap. Let us consider how big of a difference between the two candidates would be required for their confidence intervals not to overlap? Let us say that the CNN poll had Clinton in the lead by 5% (e.g., the sample percentages were 49% for Clinton vs. 44% for Trump). In this case, the 95% confidence interval for Clinton has a lower bound of 49% − 3% = 46% and Trump has an upper bound of 44% + 3% = 47%. They still overlap. Indeed, they touch even when Clinton has a 6% lead. When the difference is greater than 6%, then the confidence intervals will not overlap at any point. Roughly speaking, when the two confidence intervals do not overlap, then the difference is considered to be significant. Clinton would have to lead by over 6% points in the Florida poll for the difference to be outside the margin of error.

Note that 6% is double the 3% margin of error reported in the study. This "double the margin of error" rule is often what pollsters use to make quick, back of the envelope calculations of the margin of error for the differences between two proportions. If there are only two candidates (or only two options more generally), then this approach is adequate. When there are other candidates (think third party candidates in elections), then doubling the margin of error is a less accurate measure. Doubling the margin of error becomes less accurate the greater the support is for other third party candidates. In US presidential elections those third party votes are typically small percentages and therefore doubling the margin of error is almost always considered fine. To be precise, the formula for calculating the margin of error for the difference in two proportions is provided in the appendix (Formula A.12). Using the formula on the CNN

---

vote for Clinton when in reality they supported Trump. One possible explanation is there was the perception of a social stigma attached to voting against a female candidate in favor of a white male candidate. This hypothesis can be likened to the "Bradley Effect," which was coined after Tom Bradley, an African–American, lost the California governor's race in 1982 to a white candidate despite having a wide lead in the polls.

results leads to a margin of error for the difference in two proportions of 6.05% which of course is very close to our estimate of 6%.

One message to take away is that when comparing support for two candidates from one poll, we cannot just look at the absolute difference between two statistics. Because the statistics vary with different samples, so will the differences in those statistics. For many polls, the difference between two candidates must be more than twice the margin of error of the study in order for a candidate to have a significant lead. If you search polling results from battleground states in early November 2016, you will find that most polls suggested that no candidate had a statistically significant lead.

7.5   Summary

An important part of inferential statistics is using sample data to estimate unknown characteristics of a population. Some examples include estimating presidential approval ratings, unemployment levels, customer satisfaction levels, and tax compliance levels. In these cases, a sample of data is randomly drawn from a population and a sample statistic is calculated. Because different samples can lead to different sample statistics, we know that our estimates will likely not equal unknown parameter values. Acknowledging the difference between sample statistics and population parameters (i.e., sampling error), and by relying on the properties of sampling distributions, we can form confidence intervals around our sample statistics. Using the confidence interval formulas, we calculate an upper and lower bound. Given a 95% confidence level, for example, we can say "we are 95% confident that the interval we construct contains the unknown population value." The intuition is that, of all possible samples of a given size, only 5% will result in intervals that will not contain the true value.

We explored two forms of confidence intervals for a mean and one for a proportion. When constructing an interval around a sample mean, if the population standard deviation is *known*, then we rely on the z-distribution and the corresponding critical values. Otherwise, if we are constructing a confidence interval around a mean and the population standard deviation is *unknown*, then we rely on the t-distribution for the critical values. When constructing an interval around a sample proportion, we always use the z-distribution.

Technical Appendix

When the population standard deviation is *known*, the *margin of error* for a confidence interval around the mean is:

$$e = z_{\alpha/2}\frac{\sigma}{\sqrt{n}},\tag{A.1}$$

where $\frac{\sigma}{\sqrt{n}}$ is the standard error and $z_{\alpha/2}$ is the critical value. The subscript $\alpha/2$ is the area in each tail of the distribution and α is the level of significance.

The critical z value can be found using the z-table or found using the Excel function:

$$= NORMSINV(1 - \alpha/2),\tag{A.2}$$

where $(1 - \alpha/2)$ is the area to the left of the critical value.

The confidence interval for the mean in this case is:

$$\bar{x} \pm z_{\alpha/2}\frac{\sigma}{\sqrt{n}}.\tag{A.3}$$

When the population standard deviation is *unknown* – which defines most cases – the margin of error for a confidence interval around the mean is:

$$e = t_{\alpha/2}\frac{s}{\sqrt{n}},\tag{A.4}$$

where $\frac{s}{\sqrt{n}}$ is the estimate of the standard error and $t_{\alpha/2}$ is the critical value.

The critical t-value can be found using the t-table or found using the Excel function:

$$= T.INV(1 - \alpha/2, n - 1),\tag{A.5}$$

where $(1 - \alpha/2)$ is the area to the left of the critical value and $(n - 1)$ is the degrees of freedom.

The confidence interval for the mean in this case is:

$$\bar{x} \pm t_{\alpha/2}\frac{s}{\sqrt{n}}.\tag{A.6}$$

A binomial distribution can be approximated as normal given:

$$np \geq 10$$
$$n(1 - p) \geq 10,\tag{A.7}$$

where p is the sample proportion and n is the sample size. The standard error of the proportion is

$$\sigma_p = \sqrt{\frac{\pi(1 - \pi)}{n}},\tag{A.8}$$

where the most conservative approach is to set $\pi = 0.5$. Given a sample size n, the widest interval is estimated when the unknown value of π is set at $\pi = 0.5$. The formula for the confidence interval is therefore:

$$p \pm z_{\alpha/2} \sqrt{\frac{\pi(1 - \pi)}{n}} \quad \text{where} \quad \pi = 0.5. \qquad (A.9)$$

Note that some textbooks substitute p in place of $\pi = 0.5$, which leads to intervals that are weakly smaller (less conservative). The alternative form, when substituting p for $\pi = 0.5$, yields:

$$p \pm z_{\alpha/2} \sqrt{\frac{p(1 - p)}{n}}. \qquad (A.10)$$

To estimate the smallest sample size necessary for a desired margin of error, we can rearrange the formula for e to solve for n:

$$n = \frac{z_{\alpha/2}}{e} \pi(1 - \pi) \quad \text{where} \quad \pi = 0.5. \qquad (A.11)$$

When comparing the difference between two proportions from the same poll, we estimate the margin of error as

$$e = z_{\alpha/2} \sqrt{\frac{p_1 + p_2 - (p_1 - p_2)^2}{n}}. \qquad (A.12)$$

Table 7.2 Critical *t* values.

df	0.10	0.05	0.025	0.01	0.005
1	3.078	6.314	12.706	31.821	63.657
2	1.886	2.920	4.303	6.965	9.925
3	1.638	2.353	3.182	4.541	5.841
4	1.533	2.132	2.776	3.747	4.604
5	1.476	2.015	2.571	3.365	4.032
6	1.440	1.943	2.447	3.143	3.707
7	1.415	1.895	2.365	2.998	3.499
8	1.397	1.860	2.306	2.896	3.355
9	1.383	1.833	2.262	2.821	3.250
10	1.372	1.812	2.228	2.764	3.169
11	1.363	1.796	2.201	2.718	3.106
12	1.356	1.782	2.179	2.681	3.055
13	1.350	1.771	2.160	2.650	3.012
14	1.345	1.761	2.145	2.624	2.977
15	1.341	1.753	2.131	2.602	2.947
16	1.337	1.746	2.120	2.583	2.921
17	1.333	1.740	2.110	2.567	2.898
18	1.330	1.734	2.101	2.552	2.878
19	1.328	1.729	2.093	2.539	2.861
20	1.325	1.725	2.086	2.528	2.845
21	1.323	1.721	2.080	2.518	2.831
22	1.321	1.717	2.074	2.508	2.819
23	1.319	1.714	2.069	2.500	2.807
24	1.318	1.711	2.064	2.492	2.797
25	1.316	1.708	2.060	2.485	2.787
26	1.315	1.706	2.056	2.479	2.779
27	1.314	1.703	2.052	2.473	2.771
28	1.313	1.701	2.048	2.467	2.763
29	1.311	1.699	2.045	2.462	2.756
30	1.310	1.697	2.042	2.457	2.750
40	1.303	1.684	2.021	2.423	2.704
50	1.299	1.676	2.009	2.403	2.678
60	1.296	1.671	2.000	2.390	2.660
70	1.294	1.667	1.994	2.381	2.648
80	1.292	1.664	1.990	2.374	2.639
90	1.291	1.662	1.987	2.368	2.632
100	1.290	1.660	1.984	2.364	2.626
1000	1.282	1.646	1.962	2.330	2.581

8

Hypothesis Tests of a Population Mean

In 2010, a business professor at the University of Central Florida confronted the students in his strategic management course about cheating on a mid-term exam.[1] The class was huge, with over 600 students. The professor was convinced that roughly 200 students had cheated by getting the answers to the exam in advance. The interesting part is that he had no direct evidence. The exams were proctored in a laboratory environment and not a single student was actively caught cheating. Rather, the professor relied on statistics to drive his initial suspicion. The professor had been teaching the class for many semesters and as part of the discovery process, he conducted hypothesis tests to compare that semester's exam grades with the historic grades from past semesters. He found a significant difference. The difference was so significant that he was confident that the abnormally high grades were not due to random chance. Rather, the difference in exam grades was large enough to strongly suspect foul play. His suspicions were later confirmed by a student who tipped the professor off about students accessing the exam questions online. The guilty students eventually admitted to cheating and the entire class was required to take a new exam. While statistical analysis was not the only thing used to confirm the suspicion of cheating, the results of hypothesis testing triggered further inquiry.

The real power of statistics is being able to use samples of data to infer something unknown about a larger population. We explored one aspect of this in Chapter 7 on confidence intervals. Here, we move onto using sample data to test hypotheses regarding the larger population. We start with the simplest case in which we use one sample of data to test a single numeric value regarding the population. Some good examples are hypothesis tests for quality control of products and services. Starbucks, for example, reports that a 16 oz cup of regular coffee (the grande size of Pike Place) has 310 milligrams (mgs) of caffeine.[2] Of course, there is going to be some variation in the actual amount of caffeine

---

1 http://abcnews.go.com/Business/widespread-cheating-scandal-prompts-florida-professor-issues-ultimatum/story?id=11737137
2 https://www.starbucks.com/menu/drinks/brewed-coffee/pike-place-roast

A Guide to Business Statistics, First Edition. David M. McEvoy.
© 2018 John Wiley & Sons, Inc. Published 2018 by John Wiley & Sons, Inc.

found in every grande cup of coffee brewed across the United States and abroad. The caffeine content can depend on the water quality, how long the beans have been roasted, the age of the beans, the skillset of the barista, the type of filter, and many other things. Therefore, we would not expect every single 16 oz cup to have exactly 310 mg of coffee. Given this variation, it is possible to sample a number of cups of coffee to test whether the *average* cup of coffee has 310 mg of caffeine. Such a test could be narrowly focused on a single store or it could be more broadly focused on larger geographic regions. The sample of data would lead Starbucks to either reject the hypothesis by finding significantly more or less than 310 mg in the average cup, or fail to reject the hypothesis of 310 mg of caffeine. This is the kind of test we consider in this chapter.

8.1 Two-Tail Hypothesis Test of a Mean

Let us consider a hipster coffee company called Jittery Joe's. Ideally, they like their coffee just a tad stronger than Starbucks and target their medium (16 oz) coffee to have an average of 330 mg of caffeine. Jittery Joe's considers more than 330 mg too much and can lead to their customers getting overly anxious and irritable. Overcaffeinated customers might start flipping over tables if their muffins turn out a bit dry. Joe's also does not want to provide their customers with much less than 330 mg of caffeine, because without the right boost they may fall asleep and spend the entire day slouched over in their comfortable hipster chairs. Luckily, one of their employees named Jenny Jolt has been taking an undergraduate course in business statistics and is willing to help out the management of Jittery Joe's. She tells them she is going to take a random sample of cups over the next week and measure the caffeine content in each cup. Her goal, she explains, is to use the sample values to test whether the average amount of caffeine is different from the targeted 330 mg. The management at Jittery Joe's was excited, gave her a high five and sent her on task.

8.1.1 A Single Sample from a Population

Jenny Jolt has to decide how big of a sample she needs to take. All else equal, the more the merrier. Although the population of 16 oz coffees from Jittery Joe's is not finite (no specific number), sampling more cups would provide more information on the true average caffeine content. The trade-off, of course, is that sampling coffee is expensive. Every cup that Jenny samples is a cup that is not sold to consumers. Sampling also involves time and effort, which means more wages paid to Jenny without her contributing to coffee service. The management decides that they could afford a sample of 50 cups. Jenny is happy with that sample size. She suspects that the caffeine content from all cups served by Jittery Joe's is normally distributed. She also thinks back to her stats course and the idea of sampling distributions. That is, although she is taking only one sample of 50 cups and computing the average caffeine in those 50 cups, if she were to take many samples of size 50, the averages would be normally distributed and follow a z-distribution. Jenny, in other words, remembers the Central Limit Theorem.

Of course, Jenny Jolt will also have to estimate the standard deviation in caffeine for those 50 cups. Therefore, the distribution of average caffeine for samples of 50 cups will follow a t-distribution. Recall that when the population standard deviation is unknown, we use t in place of z when estimating a mean. The t-distribution is symmetric, mound-shaped, and looks more and more like z – the normal distribution – as the sample size goes up. Jenny, therefore, is confident that the distribution of all possible averages from samples of size 50 would look fairly normal.

Table 8.1 contains the caffeine measurements in milligrams for all 50 cups. Jenny Jolt uses a high-quality caffeine testing strip to produce her measurements. The first thing Jenny does with her 50 values is compute the mean (denoted as $\bar{x}$) and the standard deviation (denoted as s) for her sample.

Jenny calculates an average of $\bar{x} = 331$ mg and a standard deviation of $s = 3.12$ mg. Jenny also needs to estimate how much variation there would be in average caffeine for all possible samples of size 50. Recall, this is called the standard error and is calculated by dividing the sample standard deviation by the square root of the sample size ($s_{\bar{x}} = 3.12/\sqrt{50} = 0.44$ mg). Loosely speaking, the average deviation in sample mean values from 50 cups of coffee is estimated to be 0.44 mg.

Clearly, the sample mean value of 331 mg is higher than the targeted 330 mg. However, Jenny Jolt recognizes that she is working with only a sample of data

Table 8.1 Caffeine content in 16 oz cups (in mgs) for a sample of 50.

331	332	333	329	334
330	332	331	330	335
328	332	332	330	331
326	334	336	326	332
340	328	334	326	333
333	327	332	329	333
329	326	332	328	328
334	329	328	330	333
334	330	328	337	336
331	333	329	335	334

and that there is going to be variation in the sample values. If she had taken another sample of 50 cups, she might get a different average value. Therefore, what she has to determine is whether 331 mg is *far enough away* from 330 mg to conclude that the population mean is different from 330.

8.1.2 Setting Up the Null and Alternative Hypothesis

It is always a best practice to write down the hypothesis being tested. This is important because there are a few possible variations for a single sample hypothesis test. First, Jenny must decide if she is conducting a one-tail or a two-tail hypothesis test. She remembers that Jittery Joe's is concerned with both too much or too little caffeine. This suggests that a *two-tail hypothesis test* is the best option. The two-tail hypothesis just means that she is equally interested in finding if there is significantly more caffeine than the targeted 330 or significantly less, so both sides of the distribution are in play. Formally, the test looks like the following:

$$H_0 : \mu = 330$$
$$H_A : \mu \neq 330$$

The first line is called the *null hypothesis*. The null hypothesis states that the average caffeine in Jittery Joe's coffee is equal to its targeted level of 330 mg. In general, the null hypothesis is the assumed value. It can also be thought of as an established baseline. In criminal trials, for example, the null hypothesis is that the person is innocent. Or when Olympic athletes are tested for performance-enhancing drugs, the null hypothesis is that they are not using banned substances. Likewise, with quality control, the null is that the quality of the product or service is equal to the advertised levels.

The second equation is called the *alternative hypothesis*, and is often thought of as the research hypothesis. The alternative hypothesis is really what the researcher is interested in. For example, when athletes take required drug tests, the goal is to determine if they *are* using performance-enhancing drugs. Likewise, the alternative hypothesis is what Jenny Jolt wants to determine; that is, does the average cup of coffee contain an amount of caffeine different from the targeted 330 mg? The notations H_0 and H_A denote the null and alternative hypotheses for all examples throughout this text.[3]

8.1.3 Decisions and Errors

With hypothesis testing, we always report our decisions with respect to the null hypothesis. In this way, our task is simple; we can either *reject the null*

---

3 In some business statistics textbooks, the notations H_0 and H_1 are used to denote the null and alternative hypothesis, respectively.

hypothesis or we *fail to reject the null hypothesis*. If we reject the null, it means our sample data support the alternative hypothesis. In our example, rejecting the null means we find that the average caffeine level is different from 330 mg. If we fail to reject the null, it means our data support the null hypothesis that the average caffeine level is equal to 330 mg.

Before determining our decision rule, we must first explore the types of errors we could make in the process. There are two types of errors that can be made with hypothesis testing. A *Type I error* is when a null hypothesis is rejected when in reality it is correct. For example, if our sample of 50 cups leads us to conclude that the average caffeine content for all cups (i.e., the population of interest) is different from 330 mg when in reality the population average is equal to the targeted 330 mg. Recall in the chapter on probabilities, we discussed the issue of diagnosing breast cancer. Using that example, if the null hypothesis is that a patient does not have breast cancer, a Type I error would be rejecting the null when it was correct. In other words, the Type I error is diagnosing a woman with cancer when she does not have it, and in that study, there was a 7% chance of that happening.

The second type of error is called a *Type II error*, and is made when we fail to reject a null hypothesis that is actually false.[4] For example, if our sample of 50 cups leads us not to reject the null hypothesis, but in reality the average caffeine content for all cups of coffee is higher than 330 mg. In the cancer diagnosis study, the Type II error was concluding a woman does not have cancer when in reality she does. There was a 10% chance of a Type II error in that study.

Of course, a researcher, like Jenny Jolt, does not know whether the null is correct or incorrect when making the decision. If she did, then there would be no reason to conduct a test – the answer is already known. However, Jenny does have some control over the likelihood she makes an error. In particular, she has direct control over the probability of making a Type I error.

Let us first consider the state of the world in which the null hypothesis is correct and the average caffeine level is 330 mg. We know from Chapter 6 on sampling distributions that a single sample of 50 cups may not lead to an average of 330 mg even when the population average is equal to 330. This is the idea of sampling error. Remember, there is variation in caffeine levels and our sample of 50 is pretty small. However, we do know that the values of repeated samples of size 50 would be distributed symmetrically with 330 mg in the center. If the null is correct, most sample means will fall close to the 330 mg. How close? Well, if the distribution of sample means was normal, the Empirical Rule tells us that about 95% of all sample means would fall within two standard errors of 330 mg. Recall that our sampling distribution will follow a *t*-distribution and is therefore not perfectly normal. But, it is very close. In fact, with our sample size of

---

4 Some students find it useful to remember a Type II error with "*FF*" – failing to reject a false null hypothesis – and a Type I error with "*RR*" – rejecting a null hypothesis that is right.

50, 95% of all sample means would be within 2.01 standard errors from 330 mg (2.01 is found on the *t*-table in the Technical Appendix of Chapter 7). So, only 5% of all possible values would fall beyond 2.01 standard errors away from 330 in either direction. This understanding of sampling distributions and how sample mean values are dispersed around a hypothesized value is fundamental to understanding the decision rule in hypothesis testing.

We start by deciding what the threshold is for rejecting a null hypothesis. A threshold is a number that if passed triggers a rejection of the null. For a two-tail test, there is a threshold for rejection in both tails of the distribution. That is, we can reject the null because we are too far above the hypothesized 330 mg or too far below the hypothesized 330 mg. We will only reject the null, if we are far enough away from the 330 to conclude that it is unlikely that the true caffeine content is 330 mg. For instance, we could reject the null if our sample mean value is beyond 2.01 standard errors away from 330. While we know that it is possible that we could get values in this range if the null is true, it would only happen with 5% of all possible samples. In particular, 2.5% of sample means would fall in the extreme left tail and 2.5% of sample means would fall in the extreme right tail. So, if we used 2.01 as our rejection rule, we could say that if the null hypothesis is true, there is a 0.05 probability of making a Type I error. In other words, with this rejection rule, we are 95% confident that we will make the correct decision if the null hypothesis is correct. The size of the rejection region is therefore the probability of making a Type I error – we call this the *significance level* and it is denoted as α.

We decide on what the threshold for rejecting the null hypothesis is by deciding on how willing we are to make a Type I error. How willing are we to reject a null hypothesis that is correct? While in principle we could choose any level, the standards are 1%, 5%, and 10%. Whatever percentage we choose will define the threshold and the size of the *rejection region*.

8.1.4 Rejection Regions and Conclusions

To continue with our example, consider a level of significance of $\alpha = 5\%$. The thresholds for rejection in this case would be plus and minus 2.01 standard errors away from 330 mg. The ± 2.01 are critical *t* values. We can also write the critical values in terms of caffeine. If we multiple 2.01 by the standard error of 0.44, we get 0.88 mg. Therefore, the positive critical value is $330 + 0.88 = 330.88$ mg and the negative critical value is $330 - 0.88 = 329.12$ mg. If our sample of 50 cups yields an average caffeine level outside of our critical values, then we reject the null hypothesis. Figure 8.1 illustrates the rejection regions and the critical values.

We are now ready to make a conclusion. There are two ways to go about this, and if done correctly both will yield the same result. The first is to compare the critical *t* values with the sample mean value. To do so, we have to convert our

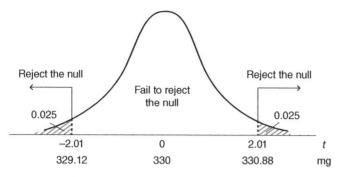

Figure 8.1 Two-tail hypothesis test critical values and rejection regions at the 0.05 significance level.

sample mean of 331 mg into a t value. We call this a *test statistic* or t_{stat} and is found by subtracting the hypothesized value of 330 from the sample mean value and dividing by the standard error (see equation A.1). Therefore, we have $t_{stat} = (331 - 330)/0.44 = 2.27$. The test statistic tells us how many standard errors 331 mg is from 330 mg. In this case, 331 mg is 2.27 standard errors greater than 330 mg. While a 1 mg difference may not seem like much, it is actually quite far away in terms of standard errors. From Figure 8.1, it is clear that the test statistic of 2.27 passed the critical t value of 2.01 and therefore we are inside the rejection region. The conclusion is to *reject the null hypothesis* at the 0.05 significance level.

Alternatively, we can compare our sample mean of 331 mg with the critical value of 330.88 mg. Since 331 > 330.88 we are inside the rejection region. One approach compares t_{stat} with $t_{critical}$ and the other compares the sample mean in mg with the critical value in mg. Both lead to the same conclusion, and so either approach is fine. An important point to remember is you need to compare apples with apples and oranges with oranges. We cannot compare t values with sample means reported in mgs.

In summary, we conclude that the caffeine level in the average cup of coffee is significantly different (more than) the targeted 330 mg. Jittery Joe's might want to address the situation or otherwise they could be dealing with an angry mob of fired-up hipsters with heart palpitations. Jittery Joe's should also recognize that there is a possibility that Jenny Jolt made a Type I error. However, if the null hypothesis is true, we would only make such an error in 5% of all possible samples of size 50.

8.1.5 Changing the Level of Significance

Suppose, we want to test the same set of hypotheses but want to limit the possibility of a Type I error to only 1% of the time. In other words, how would our test change if we conduct it at the $\alpha = 0.01$ level? At this significance level, we would be 99% confident that if the null hypothesis is true, we will make the correct decision by failing to reject it. Using our same sample, we have the same sample mean value of 331 mg and standard error of 0.44 mg. Only the critical values change. We must determine how many standard errors away from the hypothesized mean will capture 99% of the data? By the Empirical Rule, we know just about all the data is within 3 standard errors. To be precise, however, we will have to consult the t-table. We find with 49 degrees of freedom and $\alpha = 0.01$ that the critical t values are ±2.68. The picture of the test at the 1% significance level is shown in Figure 8.2.

Note again that the significance level is split evenly in both tails. Our test statistic of 2.27 is clearly in the fail to reject region, since it falls short of the 2.68 critical t value. Likewise, the sample mean value of 331 mg falls in the fail to reject region, since it does not pass the 331.18 mg critical value. Therefore, at the 1% significance level, we fail to reject the null hypothesis and find that the average cup of coffee has a caffeine level equal to 330 mg.

Comparing our two test results, we find that 331 mg is significantly different from 330 mg at the 5% significance level, but not at the 1% significance level. As a researcher, I would conclude that we find *some* evidence that caffeine levels are greater than 330 mg but not *strong* evidence. Note that, here, the only type of error that is possible is a Type II error, which would occur if the null hypothesis is actually false and we failed to reject it. While researchers do not have direct control over the likelihood of a Type II error, they can influence it indirectly. The trade-off is if the level of significance is decreased (and so too is the size of the rejection region), then the probability of failing to reject a false null hypothesis will increase. So, decreasing the probability of a Type I error increases the probability of a Type II error (the probability of a Type II error is denoted as β), holding everything else constant. In practice, businesses may find making one type of error more costly than another. The costs associated with

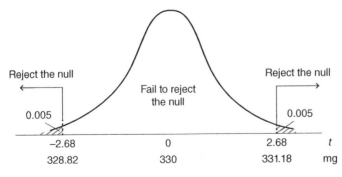

Figure 8.2 Two-tail hypothesis test critical values and rejection regions at the 0.01 significance level.

the errors depend on the context and what the response is to the conclusion of the hypothesis test. Again, consider Jittery Joe's. If rejecting the null hypothesis results in Joe's buying all new machines and retraining their entire staff, then a Type I error could be very costly (all of those new expenditures would be fixing a problem that does not exist). On the other hand, a Type II error will likely result in business as usual and they would not change anything, so it could be a very low cost error to make. However, if the caffeine-laden customers at Joe's start having medical problems and sue Jittery Joe's for gassing up their drinks, then a Type II error could come with huge costs. It all depends on the context.

8.2   One-Tail Hypothesis Test of a Mean

The most common type of hypothesis tests is two-tailed. However, there are circumstances in which a one-tail test is permissible. Consider again our hipster coffee shop Jittery Joe's and their concern about the ideal amount of caffeine. If for some reason they were only concerned about providing too much caffeine relative to the desired target of 330 mg, then they could use a one-tail test. Meaning, they would only reject the null hypothesis, if they found the average caffeine levels to be significantly greater than 330 mg. Most of the elements for completing a one-tail hypothesis test are the same as those for the two-tail hypothesis, with the exception that the rejection region is pushed entirely into one tail. For the Jittery Joe's example, it would be in the right tail.

8.2.1   Setting Up the Null and Alternative Hypotheses

The starting point for Jenny Jolt's one-tail hypothesis is to set up the null and alternative. Her research question is whether the average cup of coffee has *more than* 330 mg of caffeine. Therefore, she will frame the alternative hypothesis with a *greater than* symbol (>).

$$H_0 : \mu \leq 330$$
$$H_A : \mu > 330$$

The null hypothesis now includes the targeted 330 mg, but it also includes any level of caffeine less than the target. The reason is because with a one-tail test (right tail), we cannot reject a null hypothesis for any caffeine level we might find less than 330.[5] We have effectively narrowed our focus on only one side of the distribution. For a given level of significance, say $\alpha = 5\%$,

---

5 When visualizing or drawing the rejection region for a one-tail test, the inequality in the alternative hypothesis always points to the direction of the rejection region.

the rejection region in our right tail will be twice the size as the rejection region in the right tail in a two-tail test. Therefore, we are more likely to reject the null for sample means greater than the targeted 330 mg. It is for this reason that one-tail tests are often considered to be less conservative than two-tail tests. A more conservative approach is usually thought of as one that makes it harder to reject a null hypothesis. Think again about the example of performance-enhancing drugs in which the null hypothesis is that the athlete is clean. A one-tail test would make it easier for officials to reject the null that the athlete in question is clean. The most conservative approach is one in which innocence is presumed as the baseline and the data need to be compelling enough to reject that hypothesis.

8.2.2 Rejection Regions and Conclusions

The first step is to find the critical t value for the 0.05 significance level given a one-tail test. This is the same positive t value we would use for a two-tail test at the 10% significance level. Why? Because with a two-tail test, half of 10% is in each tail, so 5% would be in the right tail. After consulting the t-table, we locate the value as $t_{critical} = 1.68$. This means that the critical value in mg is 1.68 standard errors above 330 mg, which is $330 + 1.68 \times 0.44 = 330.74$ mg. The critical values and rejection region are illustrated in Figure 8.3.

We conclude the one-tail hypothesis test using the same approach as the two-tail test. Comparing $t_{stat} = 2.27$ with $t_{critical} = 1.68$, it is clear that the test statistic is inside the rejection region and the conclusion is to reject the null hypothesis at the 0.05 significance level. Alternatively, we can compare the sample mean of 331 mg with the critical value of 300.74 mg. Since $331 > 300.74$, the conclusion is to reject the null hypothesis. We find that the average caffeine level exceeds the targeted 330 mg.

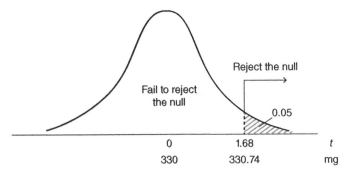

Figure 8.3 One-tail hypothesis test critical values and rejection regions at the 0.05 significance level.

8.3 *p*-Value Approach to Hypothesis Tests

In the previous sections, we considered a few different hypothesis tests using Jenny Jolt's caffeine data from her sample of 50 cups. Recall, we considered two-tail tests at both the 0.05 and 0.01 levels and a one-tail test at the 0.05 level. In all three cases, our sample statistics remained the same and only the size of the rejection regions (and hence the critical values) changed. Most importantly, the test statistic in each case was $t_{stat} = 2.27$ and we just compared it to different critical t values. Well, there is another approach to making decisions with hypothesis tests; one in which you do not have to keep referring to tables to find different critical values. This approach uses what is called a *p-value*.

The *p*-value approach starts by finding the probability of getting a test statistic that is *more extreme* than the one calculated from the sample. What does more extreme mean? It does not mean chugging four energy drinks and jumping off a plane. It simply means further into the tail of the distribution. In Jenny Jolt's case, she needs to find the probability of getting a test statistic greater than $t_{stat} = 2.27$. Since the t-distribution changes shape depending on the sample size, we do not look this value up on a table. Any stats software program can dish this out, and Excel makes it pretty easy (see A.2 for Excel formulas). Figure 8.4 illustrates the area farther into the tail than Jenny Jolt's $t_{stat} = 2.27$. This area is 0.014. For a one-tail test, the *p*-value is equal to this area, so *p*-value = 0.014. For a two-tail test, the *p*-value is double that, so *p*-value = $2 \times 0.014 = 0.028$.

The rule is: if the *p*-value < α then reject the null hypothesis.

8.3.1 One-Tail Tests

Let us start with the one-tail hypothesis test we discussed in section 8.2. We conducted that test using a level of significance = 0.05. That means the right-tail rejection region is an area of 0.05. If the *p*-value is less than the total size of the rejection region, it must be the case that the test statistic is inside the rejection region. For Jenny Jolt, the *p*-value of 0.014 is *less than* $\alpha = 0.05$, so the test

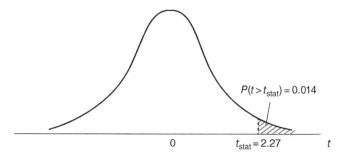

$P(t > t_{stat}) = 0.014$

0 $t_{stat} = 2.27$ t

Figure 8.4 Finding the probability of a test statistic farther into the tail than $t_{stat} = 2.27$.

statistic is inside the rejection region and she would reject the null. What is even cooler is that Jenny Jolt can quickly use the p-value rule to make a decision at any level of significance without having to find a single critical value. For example, what does Jenny conclude at the $\alpha = 0.01$ significance level? Just use the rule. Since the p-value of 0.014 is greater than 0.01, Jenny would fail to reject the null hypothesis. In fact, Jenny would reject the null hypothesis for any significance level greater than 0.014 and fail to reject for any significance level less than 0.014. This is why the *p-value is often defined as the lowest level of significance for which you would reject the null hypothesis.* A very small p-value indicates that the sample mean is very far from the hypothesized mean. Most statisticians and data analysts simply report the p-values to their results rather than stating their conclusion to a test at a given significance level. This is because an informed reader (like you after reading this section) can quickly look at the p-value and know the range of significance levels for which they would reject the null hypothesis.

8.3.2 Two-tail tests

The p-value for a two-tail test is twice that of the one-tail test. You may be asking yourself why that is the case. Well, it is because with a two-tail test, the rejection area in each tail is only half of the significance level. Remember, we divide α by 2 with these tests. So, we can either compare the one-tail p-value with $\alpha/2$ or we can double the one-tail p-value and compare it directly with α. We take the second approach. That allows us to use the same p-value rule to conclude any type of test. The rule never changes, only the calculation of the p-value changes depending on whether it is a one- or two-tail test. Jenny Jolt's p-value for a two-tail test is 0.028. She knows that she will reject the null hypothesis for any significance levels greater than 0.028, and fail to reject the null for any significance levels less than 0.028.

8.4 Summary

In this chapter, we covered how to use sample data to test a numeric hypothesis about a population mean. A sample of data was taken, the sample mean was calculated, and then compared to the hypothesized mean. If the sample mean was far enough away from the hypothesized mean, then we rejected the null hypothesis. Far enough away, however, is measured in standard errors (the average deviation of sample means), so we needed to convert the sample mean into a test statistic. The test statistic tells us how many standard errors the sample mean is from the hypothesized mean. A conclusion is made by comparing the test statistic to a critical value, or by comparing the p-value to the level of significance.

Technical Appendix

When the population standard deviation σ is unknown, we use the sample standard deviation s and the estimate of the standard error is $s/\sqrt{n}$. In this case, the distribution of all possible sample means follows a t-distribution and the *test statistic for a mean* is calculated as:

$$t_{\text{stat}} = \frac{\bar{x} - \mu_0}{s/\sqrt{n}}, \tag{A.1}$$

where $\bar{x}$ is the sample mean and μ_0 is the hypothesized mean.

The *p-value* for a one-tail or two-tail hypothesis test can be found using the following Excel formulas:

one-tail p-value $= T.DIST.RT(t_{\text{stat}}, n - 1)$

two-tail p-value $= T.DIST.2T(t_{\text{stat}}, n - 1),$ $\qquad$ (A.2)

where $2T$ indicates a two-tail test and $n - 1$ is the degrees of freedom. Although there are limited applications in the real world, most textbooks cover a hypothesis test of a mean when the population standard deviation is known. In this case, the sampling distribution can be considered normal for samples of 30 or more and the z-distribution is used. In this case, the test statistic is calculated as:

$$z_{\text{stat}} = \frac{\bar{x} - \mu_0}{\sigma/\sqrt{n}}, \tag{A.3}$$

and the p-value can be found using the z-table.

9

Hypothesis Tests of Categorical Data

In this chapter, we focus on hypothesis tests when data are categorical. Many survey questions and polls result in data that fall into this category. Each week in the United States, for example, samples of adult Americans are asked whether they approve of the way the current president is handling his responsibilities. This question is used to form the "presidential approval rating" by dividing the number that approve by the total number of respondents. Another example of categorical data is whether or not people who file their taxes get audited. A tax filing service may be very interested in publishing an estimate of the proportion of tax returns that get audited each year. Although categorical variables are not numeric, we can easily convert them into binary data. Recall, with binary data each observation (or response) can be coded as 0 or 1, where 1 is the category of specific interest. In these cases, the statistic of interest is often the *proportion* which is simply the number of 1s divided by the total number of observations.

There are two goals for this chapter. The first is to learn how to use a single sample of data to test a hypothesis concerning an unknown population proportion. To introduce the process and intuition of conducting a hypothesis test of a proportion, we will use M&M's as an example. The company Mars makes many claims about their original M&M's candies. One is captured by their famous slogan "M&M's melt in your mouth, not in your hand". While it would be possible to test this claim using a hypothesis testing approach, it is far too messy to consider seriously. Instead, we will focus on testing another one of their claims regarding the proportion of each color they manufacture. Specifically, Mars publishes that 24% of original M&M's are blue.[1] In this chapter, we will use sample data to conduct hypothesis tests regarding Mars' claim that the population proportion (π) of blue M&M's is 0.24.

The second goal is to explore hypothesis tests of categorical data when our interest is the relationship between categories from a single sample. For example, one might wonder whether there is a statistical relationship

[1] The distribution of colors for original M&M's was published on the official web site http://www .mms.com in 2011.

A Guide to Business Statistics, First Edition. David M. McEvoy.

between political party affiliation and education, or whether the survival rates from hurricanes depend on income levels. Or, to follow up with the M&M's example, whether the entire distribution of colors in a randomly drawn sample of M&M's matches the distribution of colors published by Mars. These kinds of tests are called *chi-square tests* and we will cover the basics of these as well.

We begin with a test of a single population proportion.

9.1 Two-Tail Hypothesis Test of a Proportion

Our investigation into the proportion of blue M&M's should start with a statement of the null and alternative hypothesis. Let us begin with a two-tail hypothesis test in which we are interested in proportions greater than or less than the stated 0.24. The null hypothesis in this case is Mars' manufacturing claim that the population proportion is equal to 0.24. Recall, the null hypothesis is often considered to be the established baseline. The alternative hypothesis, our research question, is that the population proportion of blue M&M's is *different from* 0.24. In equation form, this looks like the following:

$$H_0 : \pi_{blue} = 0.24$$
$$H_A : \pi_{blue} \neq 0.24$$

With a two-tail test, we can reject the null hypothesis if we find a significantly higher proportion of blue M&M's or a significantly lower proportion of blue M&M's relative to the stated 0.24.

9.1.1 A Single Sample from a Population

If we consider the population of interest an entire manufacturing run of original M&M's, we can imagine a single representative sample taken from the larger population. The sample is going to be used to either support Mars' claim that 24% of M&M's are blue or refute it. The hypothesis testing approach we are going to use assumes that the distribution of sample proportions drawn from the population is approximately *normal*. This means that if we were to take repeated samples of a certain size (with replacement) from the population, and for each sample find the proportion of blue M&M's, then the distribution of those sample proportions would be approximately normal (bell-shaped). Recall from Chapter 6 on sampling distributions that there was a test to determine if a sample size is big enough to make this assumption. The test requires that the sample size × the population proportion must be 10 or greater (see equation A.1).[2] For hypothesis testing, the hypothesized proportion is used in place of the unknown population proportion. Therefore, the distribution

---

2 Note that the normal approximation test requires that both $n\pi \geq 10$ and $n(1 - \pi) \geq 10$.

of sample proportions will be approximately normal if $n \times 0.24 \geq 10$. Simply dividing both sides of the equation by 0.24 tells us that as long as the sample size is $n \geq 41.67$ (42 M&M's or more), then we can use the normal distribution for hypothesis testing. To satisfy this, we will use a random sample of 50 M&M's to conduct our tests and we can safely assume that the sampling distribution follows a z-distribution. While a sample of size 50 is large enough, a bigger sample is almost always better. The sample results are contained in Table 9.1.

If the population proportion of blue M&M's is 0.24, then we would expect, on average, 12 out of a sample of 50 to be blue. Why? Because the expected value is $n\pi = 0.24 \times 50 = 12$. In contrast, from Table 9.1, it is found that there are nine blue M&M's out of the 50 sampled. The sample proportion is therefore $9/50 = 0.18$. Only 18% of our 50 M&M's are blue, which is of course less than the advertised 24%. Now, it is not the time to jump to conclusions. We have to look further to find out if Mars is swindling us out of delicious blue M&M's.

Remember, we are dealing with a single sample of data. If we took another random sample of 50 M&M's, we should not expect to get the same results. In fact, we can estimate how much variation we would expect in sample proportions of blue M&M's for sample sizes of 50. The average deviation in sample proportions is the standard error of the proportion and is calculated using Formula A.2. The most important element of the formula is that as the sample size goes up, the standard error goes down. Bigger samples should yield proportions closer to the population value. For a sample of 50, the standard error of the proportion is 0.06. So, while we expect 12 blue M&M's in a sample of 50, the average deviation from 12 is 3 blue M&M's ($0.06 \times 50 = 3$). Figure 9.1 provides an illustration of the sampling distribution of blue M&M's for samples of size 50, if the population proportion is 0.24.

Table 9.1 Random sample of 50 M&M's (1 = Blue; 0 = Not Blue).

1	0	1	0	1
0	1	0	1	0
0	0	1	0	0
0	0	0	0	0
0	0	0	0	0
0	0	0	0	0
0	1	0	0	0
1	0	0	0	0
0	0	0	0	0
0	0	0	1	0

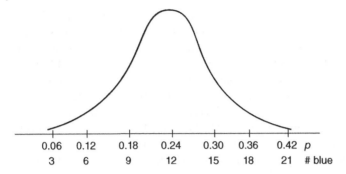

Figure 9.1 Sampling distribution of the proportion of blue M&M's for samples of 50.

9.1.2 Rejection Regions and Conclusions

We must determine whether 0.18 is far enough away from 0.24 to reject the null hypothesis that the population proportion of blue M&M's is 0.24. Let us start with a significance level of $\alpha = 0.05$, which means that if the null hypothesis is correct, we would expect to reject it (i.e., make a Type I error) only 5% of the time. The other 95% of the time, we would make the correct conclusion by failing to reject a true null hypothesis. Since we are conducting a two-tail test, half of α (i.e., 0.025) goes in each tail of the normal distribution. The critical z values for this level of significance are -1.96 and $+1.96$ (the same values used in Chapter 7 on confidence intervals). It is also possible to compute the critical values in terms of proportions. The right-tail critical value is 1.96 standard errors above the hypothesized 0.24. This yields a right-tail critical value of $0.24 + 1.96 \times .06 = 0.3576$. Likewise, the left-tail critical value is 1.96 standard errors below 0.24. This is $0.24 - 1.96 \times 0.06 = 0.1224$. The rejection regions and critical values are illustrated in Figure 9.2.

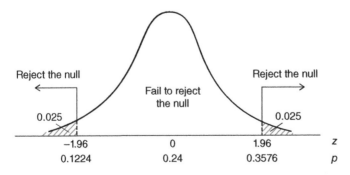

Figure 9.2 Two-tail hypothesis test critical values and rejection regions at the 0.05 significance level.

To compare the sample results with the z critical values, we need to compute the test statistic. The test statistic tells us how many standard errors 0.18 is from 0.24 (see Formula A.3). Since the standard error is 0.06, we can easily solve $z_{stat} = (0.18 - 0.24)/0.06 = -1$. So, 0.18 is 1 standard error below 0.24. z_{stat} is clearly in the *fail to reject the null* region. Alternatively, we could compare the sample proportion of 0.18 to the critical values in proportions (the second axis in Figure 9.2), in which $p = 0.18$ is also clearly in the fail to reject the null hypothesis region. Thus, at the 0.05 significance level, we find evidence in support of the null (i.e., we fail to reject the null) that the population proportion of blue M&M's is equal to 0.24.

9.2 One-Tail Hypothesis Test of a Proportion

Suppose that after years of eating original M&M's we suspected that Mars was shortchanging us on blue M&M's. We hypothesized that the actual proportion of blue M&M's is *less than* Mars' published proportion of 0.24. To answer this question, we could use a one-tail hypothesis test. Recall that the research question is framed as the alternative hypothesis while the null hypothesis captures the manufacturer's claim. The test would be set up as the following:

$$H_0 : \pi_{blue} \geq 0.24$$
$$H_A : \pi_{blue} < 0.24$$

Using a significance level of 0.05, we know that with a one-tail test the rejection region will be pushed entirely into the left side of the distribution. If you are having a hard time remembering what side of the distribution contains the rejection region, consider that the symbol in the alternative hypothesis will always point to the correct tail. The critical value can be found using the z-table and is -1.645. The rejection region and critical z value are illustrated in Figure 9.3. Notice that we also include the critical value in terms of proportions. This is found by finding the proportion that is 1.645 standard errors below the hypothesized value: $0.24 - 1.645 \times 0.06 = 0.1413$. Therefore, the hypothesis test can be concluded by either comparing the test statistic of $z_{stat} = -1$ with the $z_{critical} = -1.645$ or by comparing the sample proportion of $p = 0.18$ with the critical value (in proportions) of 0.1413. In either case, our sample statistics are not in the rejection region. We fail to reject the null hypothesis using a one-tail test at the 0.05 significance level.

With both the one-tail and two-tail tests, we fail to reject the null hypothesis. That means, we are finding support for Mars' claim that the true proportion of blue M&M's is 0.24. We make this conclusion even though our sample proportion was only 0.18. Clearly, 0.24 and 0.18 are different, but they are not different enough for us to reject Mars' claim.

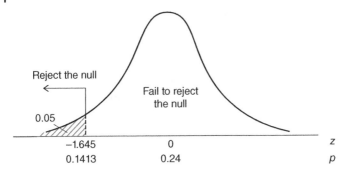

Figure 9.3 One-tail hypothesis test critical values and rejection region at the 0.05 significance level.

9.3 Using *p*-Values

The *p*-value approach to hypothesis testing was first introduced in Chapter 8. The *p*-value offers a more general way to conclude a hypothesis test by avoiding having to locate critical values for different levels of significance. For the one-tail test, the *p*-value is equal to the area farther into the tail relative to the test statistic. For the two-tail test, the *p*-value is double that area. In either case, the rule remains the same:

The p-value rule: if the *p*-value is less than α, then reject the null hypothesis.

9.3.1 One-Tail Tests Using the *p*-Value

The starting point is considering the test statistic of $z_{stat} = -1$. Given our sample, the *p*-value for the one-tail test is the area to the left of −1. This is found using the *z*-table and we get *p*-value = 0.1587. Since this area is greater than the significance level of 0.05, we fail to reject the null hypothesis. In fact, the level of significance would have to be higher than 0.1587 for us to reject the null. Since we normally only consider values for α equal to 0.10, 0.05, and 0.01, this indicates we are not really close to rejecting for any reasonable level of significance.

9.3.2 Two-Tail Tests Using the *p*-Value

If you fail to reject a null hypothesis using a one-tail test at a given level of significance, then you will certainly fail to reject the null hypothesis for a two-tail test. This is because the rejection region in each tail is going to be half the size of the rejection region in the one-tail test. A smaller rejection region means a lower likelihood of rejecting. The fact that α is divided by two is the reason why we multiple the one-tail *p*-value by two when calculating the two-tail *p*-value. This means that the two-tail test p-value is always twice that of the p-value for the one-tail test. Therefore, p-value $= 2 \times 0.1587 = 0.3174$. As is always the case, we compare the p-value directly with α. Using the rule, we would fail to reject the null for any level of significance less than or equal to 0.3174 and reject only if the level of significance was greater than 0.3174. The takeaway message is that we are not close to rejecting the null hypothesis with our sample of data.

9.4 Chi-Square Tests

In the previous sections, we covered how to use a single sample of data to test whether the unknown population proportion takes on a specific value. Here, we turn to a different set of hypothesis tests for categorical data. Our goal is not to compare a sample proportion to a given value, but rather to compare the frequencies between categories. As a motivating example, consider the following question: Is a voter's political party affiliation independent of their gender? In other words, we are interested in discovering whether there is a gender divide by party line. To answer this, we need to jointly compare the distribution of men and women in a single sample by their breakdown of party affiliation by Republican, Democrat, Independent, and others. To answer this question, we will use what is called a *chi-square test of independence*. In general, these kinds of tests will tell us whether two (or more) categorical variables are "independent" of each other. The cool (and useful) thing about these tests is that we do not have to assume anything about the shape of the populations from which samples are drawn. Chi-square tests are part of a club called *distribution-free tests*.

9.4.1 The Data in a Contingency Table

Chi-square tests of independence for two variables lend themselves nicely to contingency tables. Table 9.2 contains data from a Gallup study on gender and political party affiliation from a sample of 149,192 survey respondents. The total sample was divided evenly between men and women yielding 74,596 observations by gender.

The null hypothesis for all chi-square tests of independence is that the variables are independent and the alternative hypothesis is that the variables depend on each other. For our specific example in Table 9.2, the frequencies in each cell are clearly different by gender, but the question is are they different enough to reject the null hypothesis?

To answer this, we have to find out whether we can attribute the differences we observe to random chance or whether the differences are striking enough to conclude that the variables are dependent on each other. The first step is to ask what frequencies would we *expect* to see if the variable was indeed

Table 9.2 Observed gender and political party affiliation from a sample of n =149,192.

	Democrat	Republican	Independent	Other	Totals
Men	23871	20887	25363	4476	**74596**
Women	30584	18649	19395	5968	**74596**
Totals	**54455**	**39536**	**44758**	**10443**	**149192**

independent? Let us form an expected frequency table. First, consider that the gender of respondents in our sample is a 50–50 split. So, if gender and political party are independent, we would expect 50% of each political party affiliation to be men and the other 50% to be women. Now, just go column by column and look at the totals for political party and divide the totals equally by gender. Note if the gender divide was not even, this is no problem. Just multiply the column totals by the observed percentage. For the 54,455 total democrats in our study, we would expect 27,227.5 (or 27,228 if we round) to be males and an equal amount to be females. Likewise, for the 39,536 total republicans, we would expect 19,768 females and the same amount of males. Continuing in the same way, we arrive at the contingency table of expected frequencies in Table 9.3.

Note that the column and row totals in Tables 9.2 and 9.3 must match up. The next step is to compute a statistic that captures the total variation we have between the observed frequencies and expected frequencies. If the null were true, the differences between the observed and expected frequencies would be small. In the extreme, zero differences would be the strongest result in favor of the null. If we calculated the difference between each corresponding cell in the two tables, we would have both positive and negative differences. Since we are interested in differences in either direction, we will square those differences. As an example, consider female democrats. We observe 30,584 but we would expect 27,228 if gender and political party were independent. The difference is 3356 and if we square that difference we get 11,262,736. The last step for each cell is to get a relative measure of the difference in cells, and to do this, we take the squared difference and divide it by the expected frequency, which yields $11,262,736/27,228 = 413.45$. Then, do that for each cell so you have eight

Table 9.3 Expected gender and political party affiliation from a sample of n =149,192.

	Democrat	Republican	Independent	Other	Totals
Men	27228	19768	22379	5222	**74596**
Women	27228	19768	22379	5222	**74596**
Totals	**54455**	**39536**	**44758**	**10443**	**149192**

values in total. Then, add the values and you have the chi-square test statistic. For our example, the chi-square test statistic $\chi^2 = 1963$. At this moment, you want to pause and admire your work. Remember, if there were no differences between observed and expected frequencies, then the test statistic would be zero. Our statistic of 1963 is pretty far from zero, indicating that we will reject the null hypothesis, but we should make sure.

In order to make a conclusion we need to compare our test statistic of 1963 with a critical value. The critical value, as always, is the threshold we need to cross in order to reject the null hypothesis. It is the goal post. Chi-squared statistics are measures of variance with a lower bound of zero (because we square the differences there are no negative terms). The distribution of possibilities is right-skewed with most of the values hovering close to zero and fewer large values out into the right tail (see Figure 9.4). The exact critical value depends on the degrees of freedom and the significance level. The calculation for degrees of freedom is the number of columns−1 × the number of rows−1. In our example, we have four columns and two rows, which results in $3 \times 1 = 3$ degrees of freedom.

A table of chi-square critical values is provided in the appendix for this chapter. For a significance level of 0.05 and three degrees of freedom, the critical value is 7.815. Since 1963 is light years away from 7.815, we find strong evidence to reject the null hypothesis. The conclusion is that the gender and political party affiliation are dependent variables.

9.4.2   Chi-Square Test of Goodness of Fit

We can use the same technique of comparing the observed and expected frequencies to test whether a sample of data fits a particular kind of population. Recall the M&M's example at the beginning of this chapter. We previously focused on Mars' claim that the proportion of blue M&M's is 0.24 and learned

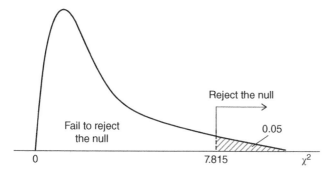

Figure 9.4 Chi-square distribution and critical value at the 0.05 significance level with three degrees of freedom.

how to test whether our sample supports this claim. Using a *chi-square test of goodness of fit*, we can jointly test whether the entire distribution of colors in our sample match the distribution Mars has published. In particular, they state that 0.13 are brown, 0.13 are red, 0.24 are blue, 0.20 are orange, 0.16 are yellow, and 0.14 are green. The null hypothesis is that the distribution is equal to these proportions. The alternative is that at least one of the proportions differs from Mars' claim.

We calculate the test statistic in the same way. We have to compare the observed frequencies with the expected ones. Consider our previous sample of 50 M&M's in which nine were blue. Table 9.4 contains the full breakdown of colors for our sample of 50 and the expected number given the posted proportions by Mars. Note that the observed numbers are different from the expected numbers. *But are they different enough for us to reject the null hypothesis?*

The chi-square test statistic is calculated in the same way as before. We find the difference between the observed and expected frequencies for each color. Take those differences and square them to get rid of the negative deviation issue. Then, divide each of the squared terms by the expected number. Let us work through the value for blue M&M's. The difference is $9 - 12 = -3$. When we square the difference we have 9, and then dividing it by 12 yields 0.75. We make the same calculations for each color. Take a shot at the calculation for orange and you should get 1.6. Now, add up your six calculated values and you have your chi-square test statistic. With our sample, it is $\chi^2 = 6.07$.

The final step is comparing the test statistic with a critical value to see if the differences are large enough to reject the null. The critical value can be found in Table 9.5 with five degrees of freedom (six categories minus one). Given a significance level of 0.05, the critical value is 11.070. Since our test statistic is less than the critical value, we fail to reject the null. Our data support Mars' claim regarding the distribution of colors in original M&M's. While we still do

Table 9.4 Number of M&M's by color in a sample of 50 and the expected number.

Color	Observed	Expected
Brown	8	6.5
Red	4	6.5
Blue	9	12
Orange	14	10
Yellow	5	8
Green	10	7
Totals	**50**	**50**

Table 9.5 Chi-square (χ^2) critical values.

Confidence:	80%	90%	95%	99%	99.9%
Signficance:	0.20	0.10	0.05	0.01	0.001
df					
1	1.642	2.706	3.841	6.635	10.828
2	3.219	4.605	5.991	9.210	13.816
3	4.642	6.251	7.815	11.345	16.266
4	5.989	7.779	9.488	13.277	18.467
5	7.289	9.236	11.070	15.086	20.515
6	8.558	10.645	12.592	16.812	22.458
7	9.803	12.017	14.067	18.475	24.322
8	11.030	13.362	15.507	20.090	26.124
9	12.242	14.684	16.919	21.666	27.877
10	13.442	15.987	18.307	23.209	29.588
11	14.631	17.275	19.675	24.725	31.264
12	15.812	18.549	21.026	26.217	32.909
13	16.985	19.812	22.362	27.688	34.528
14	18.151	21.064	23.685	29.141	36.123
15	19.311	22.307	24.996	30.578	37.697
16	20.465	23.542	26.296	32.000	39.252
17	21.615	24.769	27.587	33.409	40.790
18	22.760	25.989	28.869	34.805	42.312
19	23.900	27.204	30.144	36.191	43.820
20	25.038	28.412	31.410	37.566	45.315
21	26.171	29.615	32.671	38.932	46.797
22	27.301	30.813	33.924	40.289	48.268
23	28.429	32.007	35.172	41.638	49.728
24	29.553	33.196	36.415	42.980	51.179
25	30.675	34.382	37.652	44.314	52.620
26	31.795	35.563	38.885	45.642	54.052
27	32.912	36.741	40.113	46.963	55.476
28	34.027	37.916	41.337	48.278	56.892
29	35.139	39.087	42.557	49.588	58.301
30	36.250	40.256	43.773	50.892	59.703
35	41.778	46.059	49.802	57.342	66.619
40	47.269	51.805	55.758	63.691	73.402

(Continued)

Table 9.5 (Continued)

Confidence:	80%	90%	95%	99%	99.9%
Signficance:	0.20	0.10	0.05	0.01	0.001
df					
45	52.729	57.505	61.656	69.957	80.077
50	58.164	63.167	67.505	76.154	86.661
60	68.972	74.397	79.082	88.379	99.607
70	79.715	85.527	90.531	100.425	112.317
80	90.405	96.578	101.879	112.329	124.839
90	101.054	107.565	113.145	124.116	137.208
100	111.667	118.498	124.342	135.807	149.449

not know whether M&M's really "melt in your mouth and not in your hand", we can rest easy that we are not being misled about the color breakdown.

9.5 Summary

This chapter covered how to conduct hypothesis tests of categorical data using a single sample. We collected a sample of binary data (zeros or ones), calculated the sample proportion, and compared it to the hypothesized value. As is always the case in inferential statistics, we do not make conclusions by simply observing if our sample statistic is higher than the hypothesized value. Even if the hypothesized value were true, samples could easily be drawn from the population that yields different sample values. We have to determine if our sample value is far enough away from the hypothesized value to reject it. That is why we always compute what is called the test statistic. The test statistic tells us how many standard errors the sample value is away from the hypothesized value. We either compare the test statistic to the critical values – the thresholds into the rejection regions – or we compare the *p*-value to the level of significance.

We also considered hypothesis tests of categorical data when we are interested in comparing differences in categories from a single sample. These are called chi-square tests, and we explored the test of independence and the goodness of fit test. The test of independence is useful for many applications when you want to test whether two or more categorical variables are independent of each other. These tests can help answer questions like: is the major field of study independent of the graduation rate? The chi-square test of goodness of fit allows us to test whether the distribution of responses in a single sample match a hypothesized distribution of responses. For example, we could use this test to know whether political support is spread evenly across five candidates.

Technical Appendix

The hypothesized value for the population proportion is denoted as π_0. A sample of size n is drawn and the sample proportion, denoted as p, is calculated. The distribution of p can be assumed to be normal provided that the following two conditions hold:

$$n \times \pi_0 \geq 10$$

$$n \times (1 - \pi_0) \geq 10. \tag{A.1}$$

The standard error for the sampling distribution of p is estimated as:

$$\sigma_p = \sqrt{\frac{\pi_0(1 - \pi_0)}{n}}. \tag{A.2}$$

The test statistic for a sample proportion is calculated using the following formula:

$$z_{\text{stat}} = \frac{p - \pi_0}{\sqrt{\frac{\pi_0(1-\pi_0)}{n}}}. \tag{A.3}$$

The test statistic tells us how many standard errors the sample proportion is from the hypothesized proportion.

The *chi-square test statistic* is computed by comparing differences between observed and expected frequencies in each cell in a contingency table. If we denote R_j the total for row j where $j = (1, 2, 3, ..., r)$, and C_k the total for column k where $k = (1, 2, 3, ..., c)$. Also, let f_{jk} and e_{jk} denote the observed and expected frequencies, respectively, for each column and row. The test statistic is

$$\chi^2_{\text{stat}} = \sum_{j=1}^{r} \sum_{k=1}^{c} \frac{(f_{jk} - e_{jk})^2}{e_{jk}}. \tag{A.4}$$

10

Hypothesis Tests Comparing Two Parameters

Remember Derek "Burger" Hamburger from Chapter 7 on confidence intervals? Burger was interested in how much money he could expect to earn after graduating from college. This makes sense because Burger is going to have some hefty student loans to pay off. Suppose Burger has narrowed his choices to economics or accounting. He is debating whether he wants to be labeled a "dismal scientist" or a "bean counter."[1] Part of the decision process is a comparison of the average starting salaries between the two fields. Derek Hamburger can rely on the *hypothesis tests of two means* described in this section in order to determine if there is a significant difference in average salaries between economics and accounting.

Burger might also be interested in comparing the variability in salary amounts between the two majors. It could be the case that the averages are pretty similar, but there is more variation in one of the majors. If he is a gambling type, maybe he chooses the field with bigger risk but bigger potential reward. Or, if he is a more conservative type, he might want to choose a major with less variability in salary amounts. For this comparison, he can rely on the *hypothesis tests of two variances* described in this chapter to compare the variation in starting salaries between economics and accounting majors.

Finally, it is also possible that Burger is interested in the likelihood he actually lands a job with either a major in economics or accounting. Salary aside, Burger wants a job. In this case, Burger could compare the proportion of recent graduates who secured in jobs between economics and accounting to see if there are significant differences. To answer this question, he will lean on the *hypothesis tests of two proportions*. We will cover these in this chapter as well.

---

[1] Thomas Carlyle is credited with describing economics as the "dismal science" in the nineteenth century. The origin of the term "bean counter" is unknown.

A Guide to Business Statistics, First Edition. David M. McEvoy.
© 2018 John Wiley & Sons, Inc. Published 2018 by John Wiley & Sons, Inc.

10.1   The Approach in this Chapter

At this point in any statistics class, students and their professors begin to rely more on software programs. With multiple datasets that are often big, it is silly to use calculators or hand calculations to analyze data. Using software to compute statistics is faster, less prone to errors, and convenient. The downside is that students often begin to lose sight on what they are actually doing when they can produce results with a click of a button. The goal of this chapter is to aid in the understanding of hypothesis tests of two parameters (means, proportions, or variances). We will learn how to identify which test to run, how the software (Excel) produces the output, and how to interpret it.

10.2   Hypothesis Tests of Two Means

You may recall from the example in Chapter 7 that the record keeping of starting salaries at Burger's university is incomplete and so he will have to compare average starting salaries by relying on samples of data. The career services office has compiled two *independent samples* of data on recent starting salaries for economics and accounting graduates. The two samples are considered to be independent because each sample consists of different students. The sample of economics graduates consists of 35 observations and the accounting sample has 40. The samples do not need to be balanced for these tests, but there are some advantages in having balanced samples. We will discuss those later in the chapter. The two samples are shown in Table 10.1 (rounded to the nearest dollar).

The first thing Burger does is calculate the average salary for both majors. He finds a sample mean of $46,887.17 for economics majors and $41,895.28 for accounting majors. If Burger was naive, he may jump to the conclusion that economics majors earn more than accounting majors simply because $46,887.17 > $41,895.28. But, Burger understands that these values are from samples, and different samples will likely lead to different results. What he must determine is if the difference in the sample means is far enough away from *zero* to conclude that the average starting salaries for the entire population of economics and accounting majors are different.

10.2.1   The Null and Alternative Hypothesis

Burger starts with a two-tail test to compare the two averages. As with all hypothesis tests, he is going to use sample data to make a conclusion about the relationship between the two unknown population means (what the average earnings are for every graduate in the two majors). Therefore, his null and

Table 10.1 Starting salaries from samples of recent graduates in economics and accounting.

Economics (n = 35)		Accounting (n = 40)		
51,100	34,740	35,025	34,767	34,388
48,230	50,340	48,422	47,376	39,113
49,640	55,681	56,832	49,306	33,978
42,890	33,283	30,195	40,885	34,679
62,346	45,422	38,606	30,657	
47,013	57,147	43,430	43,908	
58,795	41,665	44,437	49,232	
38,655	45,282	52,619	35,996	
50,489	36,215	30,527	33,899	
56,504	35,523	44,334	29,977	
50,455	37,087	37,095	42,975	
36,861	59,876	39,774	54,586	
36,500	56,098	47,304	34,665	
57,324	58,951	50,371	49,547	
35,774	41,891	51,296	38,475	
53,480	40,376	32,709	50,359	
43,540	51,240	32,897	43,731	
40,638		52,033	55,406	

alternative hypothesis will contain the Greek letters μ to denote parameter values. The two-tail test will be set up as the following:

$$H_0 : \mu_{\text{econ}} = \mu_{\text{accnt}}$$
$$H_A : \mu_{\text{econ}} \neq \mu_{\text{accnt}}$$

The alternative hypothesis, which is Burger's research interest, is that the two majors have different average starting salaries. The null is that they are equivalent. Notice that unlike the single sample hypothesis tests, we studied in previous chapters there are no numbers we are testing these means against. This formulation of the hypothesis test is concerned about the *relative* values, not their absolute levels. However, we could rewrite the null and alternative hypotheses in terms of the difference between both means to form:

$$H_0 : \mu_{\text{econ}} - \mu_{\text{accnt}} = 0$$
$$H_A : \mu_{\text{econ}} - \mu_{\text{accnt}} \neq 0$$

Using this formulation, it is clear that we are testing whether the difference in population means is different from zero. All Burger has to do is determine if the difference in the two sample means ($\$46,887.17 - \$41,895.28 = \$4991.90$) is far enough away from zero to reject the null hypothesis. Once again, the level of significance will define the size of the rejection region and the test statistic will tell us how many standard errors $\$4991.90$ is away from zero. To help visualize what is going on, we can sketch out the distribution centered at zero with the two rejection regions shaded in Figure 10.1. Note that this is t-distribution. Provided that the sampling distribution of the mean for both majors follows a t-distribution, then the difference in sample means will as well.[2] Our sample sizes are above 30, so we are pretty confident that the distribution looks as that in Figure 10.1.

At this point, we want to calculate our test statistic. This will simply be the difference in the two sample means ($\$4991.90$) divided by the standard error. The calculation of the standard error, however, depends on an assumption we must make. We can either assume that the variation in salaries between economics and accounting majors is equal (i.e., we assume *equal variances of the two populations*) or we can assume that the variation in salaries is different (i.e., we assume *unequal variances of the two populations*). The assumption we make will impact the calculation of the standard error and therefore the value of the test statistic. In most cases, you will not know if the two populations of interest have equal variances. It is for that reason the safest thing to do is assume that the

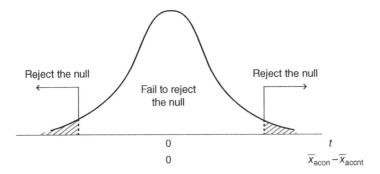

Figure 10.1 A general two-tail hypothesis test comparing two population means.

two populations of interest have unequal variances. To illustrate the differences in the calculations for our sample data, we will consider the test results under both assumptions.

10.2.2 *t*-Test Assuming Equal Variances

When we assume that the two populations have equal variances, it means we can *pool* the sample variances together. The *pooled variance* can be thought of as a weighted average of the two sample variances (see Formula A.1). The degrees of freedom for the hypothesis test are the sum of each sample size minus one. For our test, we will have $(35 - 1) + (40 - 1) = 73$ degrees of freedom. Let us take a look at the output generated by Excel for this hypothesis test conducted at a significance level of 0.05 (i.e., $\alpha = 0.05$). The specific software program is not important. All programs will yield the same statistics if using the same sample data, only the formats and labels change. The results are shown in Figure 10.2.

The first row in Figure 10.2 contains the sample means that we have already considered. The second row has the sample variances for both the economics and accounting samples. Those values are used in the calculation of the test statistic. In the next row, we have the number of observations. The pooled variance is the combined variance of both samples. The degrees of freedom (labeled *df*) are provided as well. The test statistic follows. For our samples, we have $t_{stat} = 2.6019$. The test statistic tells us that the difference in our sample means is roughly 2.60 standard errors above the hypothesized value of zero. The final four rows contain the *p*-values and the positive critical *t* values for the

	Economics	Accounting
Sample means	46887.17	41895.28
Sample variances	74353782.56	63786132.67
Observations	35	40
Pool variance	68708051.79	
Hypothesized mean difference	0	
df	73	
Test statistic (*t*)	2.6019	
p-Value (one-tail)	0.0056	
t-Critical one-tail	1.6660	
p-Value (two-tail)	0.0112	
t-Critical two-tail	1.9930	

Figure 10.2 Hypothesis test of two means assuming equal variances of the populations.

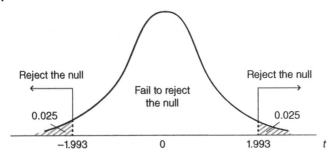

Figure 10.3 Two-tail hypothesis test comparing two population means at the 0.05 significance level and *df* = 73.

one- and two-tail test. To make a conclusion, we can either compare the t_{stat} with the critical *t* values or compare the corresponding *p*-value to the level of significance. Figure 10.3 illustrates the critical values and rejection regions for this test at the 0.05 significance level.

The test statistic of 2.60 is beyond the positive critical *t* value of 1.993. Therefore, the test statistic is inside the rejection region and we reject the null hypothesis. That is, we find evidence that the average starting salaries between economics and accounting majors are different. Economics majors appear to earn more money on average at the 0.05 significance level. The two-tail *p*-value is 0.0112 which indicates that we would reject the null hypothesis at any level of significance greater than 0.0112 and we would fail to reject the null at levels of significance lower than 0.0112. If $\alpha = 0.01$ for example, we would fail to reject the null that the average starting salaries are equal. This is fairly strong evidence that students in economics earn more on average than accounting students at their first place of employment.

10.2.3 *t*-Test Assuming Unequal Variances

With the previous hypothesis test, we assumed that the variances in starting salaries of the two populations (economics and accounting majors) were equal. This assumption allowed us to pool the two variances when calculating the test statistic and combine the samples to find degrees of freedom. In most situations (including our example), researchers cannot be confident about the relative values of two population variances. This is why in most scenarios the appropriate test to run is a hypothesis test assuming unequal variances of the two populations. In practical terms, conducting this test over the equal variance test simply means choosing the correct option from a drop down menu in a software program.

The choice will affect the calculation of the standard error and therefore the test statistic. If the two samples are of identical size, the standard errors and test statistics will be equivalent between the equal variance and unequal variance tests. In all other cases, when sample sizes are not balanced (as in our example), the standard error calculations will differ. This is because the variances are treated independently rather than pooling them together (see Formula A.3). The other impact is on the degrees of freedom.

The formula to estimate the degrees of freedom – called the Welch–Satterthwaite equation – is pretty complicated (see Formula A.3). The important point is that the degrees of freedom for the unequal variance test are lower than for the equal variance test. How does that affect the shape of the sampling distribution of the differences in the two means? Well, with lower degrees of freedom, the t-distribution is flatter with wider tails in comparison with larger degrees of freedom. In other words, the t-distribution is further away from the normal z-distribution with the assumption of unequal variances than it is with the assumption of equal variances. This will affect the calculations for p-values and could impact the resulting conclusions. If sample sizes are large enough, however, the differences are not usually dramatic. Let us look at the output in Figure 10.4 for the unequal variance test for our example with starting salaries.

Note the differences between the results from the equal and unequal variance hypothesis tests. We lose three degrees of freedom by assuming unequal variances. With 75 observations and fairly balanced samples (35 vs. 40), this difference is trivial, but it could be very meaningful with smaller or very unbalanced samples. Second, the test statistic calculation is different. $t_{stat} = 2.60$ for the equal variance test and $t_{stat} = 2.59$ for the unequal variance test. The two differences in test statistic values and degrees of freedom, though minor, interact to produce different p-values. The p-values are just slightly larger in the unequal

	Economics	Accounting
Sample means	46887.17	41895.28
Sample variances	74353782.56	63786132.67
Observations	35	40
Pool variance	68708051.79	
Hypothesized mean difference	0	
df	70	
Test statistic (t)	2.5885	
p-Value (one-tail)	0.0059	
t-Critical one-tail	1.6669	
p-Value (two-tail)	0.0117	
t-Critical two-tail	1.9944	

Figure 10.4 Hypothesis test of two means assuming unequal variances of the populations.

variance case. This translates into a slightly increased likelihood of failing to reject the null hypothesis with an unequal variance test. If the null hypothesis was false, we would be more likely to fail to reject it (higher probability of making a Type II error). Statisticians often use the term *power* to describe the chance of rejecting a false null hypothesis, and therefore unequal t-tests have less power. This is really the trade-off between the tests. As we can see, there are only marginal differences in the results for our example.

Given a significance level of 0.05, we would reject the null hypothesis that the two average starting salaries are equal between economics and accounting majors. To reach that conclusion, we either compare the two-tail p-value = 0.0117 to $\alpha = 0.05$ or we compare $t_{stat} = 2.59$ with the two-tail critical t value of 1.994. In either case, we reject the null hypothesis.

Burger finds fairly strong evidence that economics majors make more money on average than accounting majors at their first place of employment.

10.2.4   One-Tail Hypothesis Tests of Two Means

While two-tail tests are by far the more frequent, it is easy to compute a one-tail hypothesis test using the same output. Of course, if we reject the null hypothesis at the 0.05 level using a two-tail test, then we will certainly reject a null hypothesis using a one-tail test. This is because the rejection region in the relevant tail will be twice the size in relation to the two-tail test. To illustrate, consider the p-value for the one-tail test in the unequal variance test in Figure 10.4 which is p-value = 0.006. Note, as always, this is half the size of the p-value for the two-tail test. Consider the following one-tail hypothesis test of whether the average starting salary of economics majors is *greater than* that of accounting majors:

$$H_0 : \mu_{econ} \leq \mu_{accnt}$$
$$H_A : \mu_{econ} > \mu_{accnt}$$

We would reject the null hypothesis for any level of significance higher than the p-value = 0.006 and fail to reject the null for any significance level lower than 0.006. Thus, Burger can conclude that the average starting salary of economics majors is higher than the average starting salary of accounting majors at the 0.01, 0.05, and 0.10 significance levels using a one-tail test.

10.2.5   A Note on Hypothesis Tests Using Paired Observations

For a brief moment, let us turn away from the starting salary example. Instead, suppose we were interested in determining the effect caffeine has on average sleep time. There are different ways such a test could be conducted. We could use two different independent samples of people, and in one sample their sleep duration is measured without the use of caffeine and in the other sample their sleep duration is measured under the influence of caffeine. If the samples are randomly drawn from the same population, then we could use either of the tests (equal or unequal variance t-tests depending on our assumptions) previously described in this chapter.

However, if the study used the same sample of people to measure their sleep both before caffeine and after caffeine, then those observations are paired (often called *dependent samples*). In this case, it would not be appropriate to treat the before and after measures as if they were drawn from two independent populations. Rather we would like to run a t-test using paired observations. While most textbooks include this test in the chapter on two sample tests, it is really a single sample hypothesis test and therefore the mechanics of the test have already been covered in Chapter 8. The only difference is that the single sample of data is now the *difference* in the before and after measures. The degrees of freedom are the number of pairs minus one. To illustrate, consider the partial dataset in Table 10.2.

The first column in Table 10.2 is the subject's name. The second column is the hours they slept for a day without consuming caffeine. The third column shows how many hours each subject slept when consuming caffeine and the final column, labeled d, is the difference between the two.

A two-tail hypothesis test comparing the average sleep time with and without caffeine could be written as:

$$H_0 : \mu_d = 0$$
$$H_A : \mu_d \neq 0$$

This formulation of a hypothesis test is the same as we considered in Chapter 8. To conclude the test, we only have to consider the data from the last column in Table 10.2 as a single sample. Therefore, the t-test for paired observations is no different from a single sample t-test.

Table 10.2 Hours of sleep for the same participants with and without consuming caffeine in the day.

Participant	No caffeine	With caffeine	d = difference
Carolyn	6.14	5.43	0.71
Steve	6.35	6.43	−0.08
Olive	5.89	4.87	1.02
Tim	7.34	7.01	0.33
Michele	7.21	6.51	0.7
Marta	6.34	5.87	0.47

10.3 Hypothesis Tests of Two Variances

In the earlier sections of this chapter, we were interested in comparing the average salaries between two majors. Part of that process was making an assumption regarding the relationship between the variance in starting salaries between the majors. In this section, we will directly test those variances. The goal is to find out if the variation in starting salaries is different between the two majors Derek Hamburger is considering. Burger, for example, may want to choose a career with less volatility in starting salary amounts.

Many statisticians (and statistics textbooks) are inclined to first conduct a hypothesis test of the variances and use that result to inform which test to run to compare the means. This two-step hypothesis test approach is usually not recommended because every additional test that is conducted will reduce the degrees of freedom (and thus the power of the test). For this reason, we consider the test of variances independent of the test of means.

Let us consider a two-tail test of the population variances. The null and alternative hypotheses would be framed as the following:

$$H_0 : \sigma^2_{econ} = \sigma^2_{accnt}$$

$$H_A : \sigma^2_{econ} \neq \sigma^2_{accnt}$$

If the null hypothesis is rejected, then Derek finds evidence that the two majors have different variances in starting salaries. Otherwise, failing to reject the null indicates that the variances are the same. It will be useful to rewrite the null and alternative in terms of a ratio of the two unknown population variances. This is because it turns out that the test statistic for this test is the ratio between the two sample variances. In this way, this test is reasonably straightforward. Dividing both sides by the term on the right-hand side of the null and alternative yields:

$$H_0 : \frac{\sigma^2_{econ}}{\sigma^2_{accnt}} = 1$$

$$H_A : \frac{\sigma^2_{econ}}{\sigma^2_{accnt}} \neq 1$$

The interpretation of the null is that if the two populations have the same variance, then the ratio should be equal to 1. The focal point of one is important. If the ratio of our two sample variances (s^2_i / s^2_j) is far enough away from one in either direction, then we will reject the null. Again, *far enough away* is based on a choice of the significance level.

It is here that we introduce another sampling distribution. For this test, the distribution of the ratio of two sample variances (s^2_i / s^2_j) will not be symmetric or mound-shaped. Rather, it is right-skewed and follows what is called an

F-distribution, named after Ronald Fisher (1890–1962). We also call this hypothesis test an *F-test*. As always, for a two-tail test, we divide the level of significance equally into both tails of the distribution. The critical values will depend on the degrees of freedom which is $n - 1$ for each sample size. There are 34 degrees of freedom for the sample of economics majors and 39 for accounting majors. Most statistics textbooks provide tables to look up critical values for the F-test. There are different tables for different levels of significance and each table has a limited range of degrees of freedom to look up. For this reason, it is better to rely on a software program to generate the critical values (and the p-values) for an F-distribution (the Excel formulas can be found in (A.7)).

Let us start by sketching out the sampling distribution, rejection regions, and critical values for our example. In Figure 10.5, the notation F_L and F_R indicates the left- and right-tail critical values. We will get to those in a minute. The test statistic is the ratio of the two sample variances. Those two values can be found very easily, and they have already been calculated for us in Figures 10.2 and 10.4. The sample variance for economics majors is 74,353,782.56 and is 63,786,132.67 for accounting majors. Remember those values are in dollars squared. Clearly, the sample variance for economics majors is higher. The question we ask: *is the difference large enough to conclude that the population variances are different?*

To construct the test statistic, we simply divide one sample variance by the other. But which one goes in the numerator? To simplify the analysis, we will conduct what is called a *Folded F-test* and we will always put the larger sample variance in the numerator and divide it by the smaller sample variance. What this does is restrict our attention to the right side of the distribution because the test statistic cannot be less than one. This is called the Folded F-test because the left-hand side of the distribution is now out of play and it could be represented by folding back the part of the F-distribution less than one, so that it is no longer in sight (see Figure 10.6). The folded $F_{stat} = s^2_{econ}/s^2_{accnt} = 1.17$. The interpretation is that the sample variance in salaries for economics majors

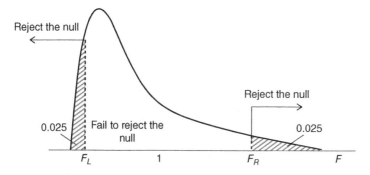

Figure 10.5 Two-tail F-test of two population variances at α=0.05.

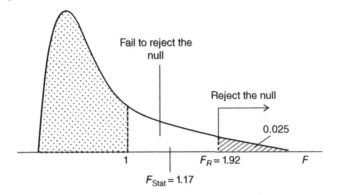

Figure 10.6 Folded F-test of two population variances at $\alpha=0.05$.

is 1.17 times the sample variance for accounting majors. To make a decision regarding whether 1.17 is far enough away from the hypothesized value of 1, we can either compare the F_{stat} to the right-tail critical value F_R or compare the p-value to α.

Using an Excel function (see Formula (A.7)), the right-tail critical value is $F_R = 1.92$. Since $F_{stat} < F_R$, the conclusion is to fail to reject the null hypothesis. Therefore, we find evidence that the variance in starting salaries is equal between economics and accounting majors at the 0.05 significance level. We can also rely on computer software to generate the p-value. The p-value is the lowest level of significance for which we would reject the null hypothesis. Using Excel (Formula (A.7)), the p-value = 0.3202. Therefore, the null hypothesis would only be rejected for significance levels greater than 0.3202. Since we are typically considering levels ranging from 0.01 to 0.10, the conclusion is to fail to reject the null hypothesis. The two majors have equal variation in starting salaries.

10.4 Hypothesis Tests of Two Proportions

Thus far, we have discussed methods of comparing the means and the variances of starting salaries between economics and accounting majors. However, our protagonist Derek Hamburger may also be interested in comparing the proportion of graduates who actually secure in jobs. For instance, it may be that economics graduates who find employment earn more than their accounting peers, but accountants have an easier time finding jobs. If Burger is thinking about his expected starting salary, he will have to consider the likelihood of finding employment as well as average earnings.

To do this, he gets his hands on two different samples from the career services department. For both samples, 100 former students were surveyed to determine whether they found employment three months after graduating. For the sample of economics students, 70 out of 100 students found jobs, which is a sample proportion of $p_{econ} = 0.70$. For the sample of accountants, 90 out of 100 found jobs yielding $p_{accnt} = 0.90$. Burger is learning that because he is dealing with sample data he cannot simply compare 0.70 with 0.90 to make a broad conclusion. He has to determine if this absolute difference of 0.20 is statistically different from zero.

As in the previous chapters, distributions of binary data can be assumed to be normal as long as long as the sample sizes are large enough (see Formula (A.1) in Chapter 7). Since both samples are large enough to satisfy this constraint, we know that the difference in the two samples is also normal. Therefore, the appropriate sampling distribution for the difference in proportions $(p_{econ} - p_{accnt})$ is the z-distribution.

Given a two-tail test, Derek Hamburger can form the null and alternative hypothesis as:

$$H_0 : \pi_{econ} = \pi_{accnt}$$
$$H_A : \pi_{econ} \neq \pi_{accnt}$$

The null states that the two population proportions are equal (or, alternatively, that the difference in the two population proportions is equal to zero). The alternative states that the proportion of students who find jobs is different between majors. Suppose the test is conducted at a significance level of 0.05. As we are now familiar with the z-distribution, we can sketch out the rejection region and critical values for our test (see Figure 10.7). Recall that the z-distribution is not dependent on the number of observations. The critical values in this case are the familiar -1.96 and 1.96. The hypothesized difference of zero is at the center of the axis for the difference in the two proportions.

The test statistic – z_{stat} – is calculated by taking the difference in the two sample proportions $p_{econ} - p_{accnt} = -0.20$ and dividing by a standard error. The formula for the test statistic can be found in A.8. z_{stat} tells us how many standard

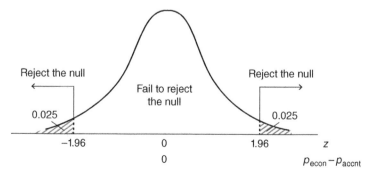

Figure 10.7 Hypothesis tests of two proportions at $\alpha = 0.05$.

errors the difference of -0.20 is from 0. Using A.8, we get $z_{stat} = -3.54$ which is well beyond the left-tail critical value of -1.96. So, the difference between the two sample proportions is 3.54 standard errors below zero. Our knowledge of the Empirical Rule comes in handy here. We know that with a normally distributed dataset almost 100% of the data will fall within three standard errors of the center. Therefore, 3.54 is convincing evidence that the null hypothesis is false and should be rejected. If the null were true, sample sizes like ours would lead to test statistics more extreme than 3.54 about 0.04% of the time. Recall, the p-value is found by finding the area less than -3.54 on the z-table and doubling that value. This results in a p-value $= 0.0004$. We reject the null hypothesis that the two proportions are equal for levels of significance greater than 0.0004.

Derek Hamburger has strong evidence that the proportion of graduates who find jobs within three months of graduation is higher for accountants than for economists.

10.5 Summary

In this chapter, we discussed how to conduct hypothesis tests for comparing two parameter values. There are many situations in which these tests can prove useful. Some examples include comparing the effectiveness of two marking strategies, comparing the speed of two wireless internet providers and comparing customer satisfaction rates between two insurance providers. We explored how to conduct hypothesis tests comparing two means, proportions, and variances. In all cases, a sample of data was drawn from each population of interest and the two samples were compared to make inferences about the relationship between two unknown population parameters. When comparing two means using independent samples, we either assumed that the two populations had equal variances or we made the more conservative assumption that the two populations had unequal variances. The main differences in the two approaches appear in the calculation of the test statistic and the degrees of freedom.

Technical Appendix

When conducting a t-test of two means *assuming equal variances* of the two populations, the formula for the test statistic is

$$t_{\text{stat}} = \frac{\overline{x}_1 - \overline{x}_2}{s_p \sqrt{\frac{1}{n_1} + \frac{1}{n_2}}}, \tag{A.1}$$

where $s_p \sqrt{\frac{1}{n_1} + \frac{1}{n_2}}$ is the standard error, and the pooled variance is:

$$s_p^2 = \frac{(n_1 - 1)s_1^2 + (n_2 - 1)s_2^2}{n_1 + n_2 - 2}. \tag{A.2}$$

The degrees of freedom for the t-test assuming equal variances is $n_1 + n_2 - 2$.

When conducting a t-test of two means *assuming unequal variances* of the two populations, the formula for the test statistic is

$$t_{\text{stat}} = \frac{\overline{x}_1 - \overline{x}_2}{\sqrt{s_1^2/n_1 + s_2^2/n_2}}, \tag{A.3}$$

where $\sqrt{s_1^2/n_1 + s_2^2/n_2}$ is the standard error, and the Welch–Satterthwaite formula for the degrees of freedom is

$$df = \frac{[s_1^2/n_1 + s_2^2/n_2]^2}{\frac{(s_1^2/n_1)^2}{n_1 - 1} + \frac{(s_2^2/n_2)^2}{n_2 - 1}}. \tag{A.4}$$

With two dependent samples (e.g., before and after studies), we rely on a t-test on the paired observations. The difference between the before and after measure is denoted as d and the average difference is denoted as $\overline{d}$. The test statistic is:

$$t_{\text{stat}} = \frac{\overline{d} - 0}{s_d/\sqrt{n}}, \tag{A.5}$$

where s_d is the standard deviation of the variable d. When conducting a folded F-test of *two population variances*, the test statistic is calculated as

$$F_{\text{stat}} = \frac{s_{\text{big}}^2}{s_{\text{small}}^2}, \tag{A.6}$$

where s_{big}^2 is the larger of the two sample variances. To find the right-tail critical value for the folded F-test, and the associated p-value, we can use the following two Excel formulas:

$$F_R \text{ in Excel} = F.INV.RT(\alpha/2, n_1 - 1, n_2 - 1)$$

$$p\text{-value for } F_{\text{stat}} \text{ in Excel} = F.DIST(F_{\text{stat}}, n_1 - 1, n_2 - 1), \tag{A.7}$$

where $F.INV.RT$ is the formula for the critical value and $\alpha/2$ is the area in the right-tail rejection region.

When conducting a z-test of *two proportions*, the test statistic is calculated as

$$z_{\text{stat}} = \frac{p_1 - p_2}{\sqrt{\hat{p}(1 - \hat{p})(1/n_1 + 1/n_2)}} \tag{A.8}$$

where $\hat{p} = \dfrac{x_1 + x_2}{n_1 + n_2}$.

11

Simple Linear Regression

You may be surprised to learn that not all students love taking courses in statistics. Hard to imagine right? The first day of the semester I ask students to raise their hand if they are taking my statistics class as an elective, simply because they are interested in the topic. In over 20 semesters, I have not witnessed a single hand raised. Perhaps, there are dozens of keen students who are just too embarrassed to raise their hands. Or, perhaps, students take statistics only because they have to fulfill a requirement for their major. (I have decided not to investigate this further and leave open the possibility the former explanation is true.) Anyway, I usually follow this with a discussion of the course syllabus, the required assignments, and how grades are determined. During the first class I also cover the issue of class attendance.

I often teach fairly large statistics courses and as the semester rolls on attendance rates seems to always fade. In that first class, I try to convey to my students the importance of attending class in order to learn the material and ultimately do well on the assignments. I tell my students that there are many factors that can influence how well they will do in my course, but class attendance is the strongest predictor. We discuss the potentially important role of other factors like major, hours dedicated to studying, SAT scores, whether they have jobs, whether they are involved in athletics, and many others. While some of these factors are important predictors of performance in the class, I stress that attendance is the most important factor. To bolster the point, I emphasize that I am not guessing. Using previous semesters as samples, I have found that on average the more classes a student attends the better they do in the course. I make this claim because I rely on what is called regression analysis to tease out the relationship between one variable (course grade) and other variables (attendance). Regression analysis is the topic of this chapter and the next two.

In this chapter, we will cover what is called *simple linear regression*. It is *simple* in the sense that we only consider two variables – often referred to as a bivariate relationship – and the goal is to estimate the effect changing one variable (e.g., attendance rate) has on another variable (e.g., course grades). In reality, simple linear regression is in most cases too simple. There are often many things

A Guide to Business Statistics, First Edition. David M. McEvoy.
© 2018 John Wiley & Sons, Inc. Published 2018 by John Wiley & Sons, Inc.

that can affect the value of a single variable. The next chapter will cover multiple regression, but for now, we will start with the simplest case. The advantage is that we can learn the mechanics and interpretations of regression analysis in a stripped-down setting and we can build on this in the next chapter. Let us get into it.

11.1   The Population Regression Model

The starting point is having a theory about the relationship between two variables. Do not get put off by the word theory. It does not have to be anything fancy, just a conjecture about the relationship between two variables, which is logically based. Keeping with our example, my theory might be that if students attend more classes, they will be exposed to more of the material and can do better on assessment activities. In this simple theory, I assume that course grades, in part, *depend on* attendance rates and not the other way around. In this case, course grade is the *dependent variable* and the attendance rate is the *independent variable*. Notationally, we use Y to denote a dependent variable and X to denote independent variables. In general, we say that Y is a function of X. The independent variable X is also often referred to as the *explanatory variable* because it is hypothesized that X explains changes in Y.

The *linear* part of simple linear regression now comes into play. We assume that there is a linear relationship between Y and X, but we also acknowledge that there is a random element in explaining changes in the dependent variable. The linear part is the structural or deterministic part and the random part is exactly that, random. Specifically, with simple linear regression, we assume that the relationship between Y and X takes the following form:

$$Y_i = \beta_0 + \beta_1 X_i + \varepsilon_i$$

The equation above is called the *population regression model*. The subscript i denotes individual values for X. The $\beta_0 + \beta_1 X_i$ is the linear component and ε_i is the random component at each value of the independent variable. The two β terms and ε are population parameters (the Greek letters always indicate this). We will never actually observe these parameter values. The best we can do is use sample data to estimate them. This is the goal of regression.

The first term β_0 is a constant term that is independent of values for X. The second term $\beta_1 X_i$ captures the influence the independent variable X_i has on the dependent variable. We call ε_i the error term. The error term, in part, captures variables other than our X variable, which influence Y and are not included (i.e., omitted variables). It also captures unobservable shocks in the relationship between Y and X that are modeled as random. With simple linear regression, we make quite a few important assumptions about the error term. The first one is that the error term on average is equal to zero. The idea is that there are deviations from the linear component of the population regression model, but the positive deviations cancel out the negative deviations and on average the term is equal to zero. This assumption allows us to rewrite the population regression model in terms of its expected value (or average relationship). Using the assumption that the error term is on average zero, we can form:

$$E[Y_i] = \beta_0 + \beta_1 X_i$$

This equation can be interpreted as the average relationship between Y and X. Since we assume $E[\varepsilon_i] = 0$, the random part drops out. This equation is what we can estimate using samples of data. This equation is clearly linear. It follows the recognizable $y = mx + b$ definition of a line. At the end of the day, we are going to end up with a line that contains an estimate for the constant term β_0 which is the intercept and an estimate of β_1 which is the slope. In this format, β_1 is the change in Y caused by a one unit increase in X. Since we will never observe the β terms directly, we have to estimate them with sample statistics.

To differentiate between parameters and statistics, we denote the estimate of the average relationship between X and Y as:

$$\hat{Y}_i = b_0 + b_1 X_i$$

$\hat{Y}_i = b_0 + b_1 X_i$ is called the *sample regression function*. The notation $\hat{Y}_i$ denotes the average estimate of Y for a given X_i. The term b_0 is the estimate of the intercept and b_1 is the estimate of the slope. Now, we turn to how we actually get numeric values for b_0 and b_1 using a sample of data.

11.2 A Look at the Data

The starting point is drawing a sample of data that can be used to estimate the relationship between the two variables. The sample should be representative of the population of interest. For example, if the population of interest is all college students in the United States taking a course in statistics, then the sample should reflect that population. If our population is more narrow, for example, students taking my statistics course in Boone, North Carolina, then the sample should represent that population. For our purposes, we will use course grades and attendance from a previous class. The sample of data is contained in Table 11.1. The bold values are the student observation numbers, the Y-values are percentage grades, and the X-values are the number of classes (out of 16) that the student attended.

To get a better feel for the relationship between course grades and attendance, we can form a scatterplot. Each diamond on the scatterplot in Figure 11.1 is a single student's pair of course grade and attendance. The scatterplot is useful for illustrating patterns in the data. While there is a noticeable positive trend in the data, it is clear that there is not a one-to-one relationship between course

Table 11.1 Sample data from 40 students of their course grade (Y) and the number of classes attended (X).

ID	Y	X	ID	Y	X
1	61	10	21	86	9
2	69	9	22	87	12
3	75	10	23	88	8
4	76	10	24	88	14
5	76	8	25	89	12
6	79	10	26	89	12
7	79	11	27	90	13
8	79	7	28	90	12
9	81	14	29	90	12
10	82	6	30	91	13
11	83	12	31	91	12
12	83	10	32	92	14
13	84	13	33	93	13
14	84	10	34	94	14
15	84	9	35	94	14
16	84	6	36	94	11
17	84	10	37	95	16
18	84	16	38	95	11
19	85	12	39	95	15
20	86	11	40	98	16

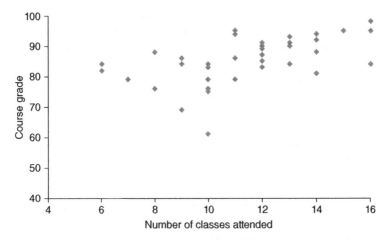

Figure 11.1 Course grades (Y) versus classes attended (X).

grade and attendance. Before estimating the sample regression function, it is sometimes informative to calculate how linear the sample data are. This can be achieved by calculating the Pearson *correlation coefficient*, which is denoted as r. If the measure for $r = 1$, it means that there is a positive one-to-one relationship between X and Y. In other words, any change in Y can be completely accounted for by a change in X. When $r = 1$, the relationship between the two variables is perfectly linear with a positive slope. Alternatively, $r = -1$ indicates a perfect linear relationship with a negative slope. Using Formula A.1, the correlation coefficient for our data is $r = 0.55$. This confirms that although there is some degree of linearity in the relationship between course grade and attendance, there is a great deal of variation unexplained by attendance.

11.3 Ordinary Least Squares (OLS)

The objective is to choose the best line to fit the data illustrated in Figure 11.1. For our purposes, the "best" line is the one that minimizes the distances between the points on the scatterplot and the regression line. The difference between the estimate of Y – which is $\hat{Y}_i$ – and the actual value of Y for a given X is called the *residual*. It can be expressed as $e_i = \hat{Y}_i - Y_i$. The residuals (e_i's) are our estimates of the unobserved random errors (ε_i's). The best fit line is the one that minimizes the residuals. However, because we will have data points above and below the chosen regression line, we will have both positive and negative residuals. To treat positive and negative residuals with equal footing, we square them. The criteria we use to find our best fit line is called *ordinary least squares* or *OLS*. Using OLS, the "best" fit regression line is the line that minimizes the sum of the squared residuals.

Now that we know the criteria used to define the best line, we can solve for the values of b_0 and b_1 that achieve this goal. Undergraduate courses in business statistics do not have students derive these formulas, they are simply presented. However, it is useful to consider where they come from. The starting point is expressing the residuals in terms of the intercept and slope estimates. Since $e_i = \hat{Y}_i - Y_i$, we can rewrite the residuals as $e_i = b_0 + b_1 X_i - Y_i$ and then square the residuals to form $e_i^2 = [b_0 + b_1 X_i - Y_i]^2$. Now, we have an equation for the squared residuals as a function of the intercept and slope estimates. We can then use a bit of calculus to minimize the sum of the squared residuals (the OLS criteria). The result will be two equations that can be solved jointly to find the unique values for b_0 and b_1 that form the best fit line. See Formulas A.2 and A.3.

In practice, statisticians do not calculate regression equations by hand. Every statistics software program has a tool that can estimate the sample regression function. In Excel, the tool is called "regression" and is found in the data *Analysis Toolpak in Excel*. For most versions of Excel, the Analysis Toolpak comes standard with the program and simply needs to be activated. You can find many instructional videos online that walk you through this.[1] Using our sample of data on course grades and attendance, the output from the regression tool in Excel is contained in Figure 11.2.

Many statistics are included in the output in Figure 11.2, but for the moment let us concentrate on the values for b_0 and b_1, which are our best estimates of the unknown parameters β_0 and β_1. Those are found in the bottom-left corner under the column labeled "Coefficients." The intercept is $b_0 = 67.02$ and the slope is $b_1 = 1.63$ (rounded to two decimal places for convenience). Putting it together, we have the following sample regression function for our data:

$$\hat{Y}_i = 67.02 + 1.63X_i$$

This sample regression function is the line that minimizes the sum of the squared residuals. The slope estimate of 1.63 tells us that as the number of classes attended increases by one unit (i.e., one class), the average estimate of the course grade increases by 1.63 units (i.e., percentage points). In other words, for every additional class, a student attends the predicted effect is, on average,

Regression statistics	
Multiple R	0.5503
R square	0.3028
Adjust R square	0.2845
Standard error	6.4261
Observations	40

ANOVA					
	df	SS	MS	F-stat	p-value
Regression	1	681.56	681.56	16.50	0.0002
Residual	38	1569.21	41.30		
Total	39	2250.78			

	Coefficients	Standard error	t-stat	p-value	Lower 95%	Upper 95%
Intercept	67.0249	4.7018	14.2553	0.0000	57.5067	76.5432
X (classes attended)	1.6324	0.4018	4.0626	0.0002	0.8190	2.4458

Figure 11.2 Regression output for course grades as a function of classes attended.

1 Here is one for Excel 2016 for Windows: https://www.youtube.com/watch?v=mIoS7IRo36c

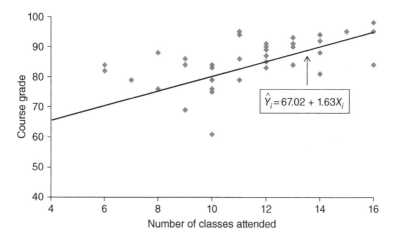

Figure 11.3 Scatterplot of course grades and attendance with the fitted regression line.

a 1.63 percentage point higher course grade. With regression, it is very important to know what units the data are in for both Y and X in order to correctly interpret the results. Also, note that the slope estimate of 1.63 is just a point estimate. That estimate is based on one single sample, and that estimate is likely to change with different samples. Just as in Chapter 7, we can construct confidence intervals around our estimates. The formula can be found in A.6

One useful thing we can do with the sample regression function is use it to *predict* the average value for the dependent variable given a value for the independent variable. Suppose for example a student is interested in using these results to predict a course grade for attending only seven classes. Plugging in $X = 7$ into the equation yields $\hat{Y} = 67.02 + 1.63(7) = 78.43$, which is a C+. With prediction using the simple linear regression, it is important to remember that it is not typically appropriate to plug in values for X, which are outside of the range from our dataset. Meaning, the range in attendance values in our data is 4–16 classes. We would not want to plug in values higher than 16 or lower than 4, because we have no idea what the bivariate relationship is in those ranges. For this reason, the intercept (e.g., 67.02) cannot be interpreted as the expected value for Y when $X = 0$ *unless* the independent variable takes on a value of zero in our sample data. For our data, the only relevant part of the regression line is the segment between 4 and 16 classes attended. In Figure 11.3, the fitted regression line is included with the scatterplot on course grades and attendance.

11.4 The Distribution of b_0 and b_1

Thus far, we have used our sample of 40 observations to estimate the underlying relationship between course grade and attendance in my business statistics course. Of course, if I was to draw another sample with different students, I am likely to get different estimates for the intercept and slope. They might be close, but they will differ. The point is that b_0 and b_1 are random variables and will have their own distributions (i.e., their own shape, mean, and standard deviation). It turns out that under certain conditions, the sampling distributions of these statistics follow a t-distribution. That is, they are symmetric and mound shaped. The center of the distribution is the average value which will equal the true parameter value (i.e., the βs). You may recall that when the average of a sample statistic equals the population parameter, we call that statistic an unbiased estimator. These properties rely on us making a few more assumptions about the random component in the relationship between X and Y. Let us list all the assumptions:

- **Assumption 1:** The random errors equal zero on average.
- **Assumption 2:** The random errors are normally distributed.
- **Assumption 3:** The random errors have constant variance (constant variance is called *homoskedastic*).
- **Assumption 4:** The random errors are independent of each other.

We will cover some of the implications of violating these assumptions later in this chapter, but for now let us discuss their meaning. Assumption 1 we have already introduced. Recall, that was the assumption that positive errors cancel out negative errors, so on average the errors equal zero. Assumption 2 is about the shape of the distribution of random errors. We not only assume that positive deviations cancel out the negative deviations (Assumption 1), but also assume that the shape of those deviations is normal. Meaning, if we created a histogram with all of the error terms, it would take on a normal shape. Assumption 3 is often called the assumption of *homoskedasticity* of the random errors. The meaning is that at every value of the independent variable, the variability in the random errors is the same. There is not, for example, more variation in errors with higher values for X. If that were the case, Assumption 3 would be violated and the variance in the error term would be considered *heteroskedastic*. The fourth assumption is that the random errors associated with one X value are not a function of the random errors for another X value. They are, by this assumption, truly random and independent across all X values.

Given that these assumptions hold, we can say that the distributions for b_0 and b_1 are t-distributions that are centered at β_0 and β_1, respectively. Recall that the standard deviation of a sampling distribution is called a standard error. The standard errors for b_0 and b_1 are the estimates of the average deviations around the true parameter values. These standard errors are calculated for us in the regression output and we will analyze them shortly.

11.5 Tests of Significance

Using the OLS regression, we estimated a 1.63 percentage point increase in the course grade for every additional class attended. While a 1.63 percentage point increase for every class attended sounds pretty significant, we cannot say for sure without an appropriate comparison. The comparison we make in regression is relative to zero. Imagine, for example, a variable that likely has zero influence on a student's course grade. The length of a student's hair comes to mind. If I gathered a sample of data on course grades and student hair length and I ran a regression analysis, I could get an estimate of b_1 which would be interpreted as the expected change in the course grade caused by a one-unit increase in hair length. Even if the true underlying relationship between the two variables is zero (i.e., $\beta_1 = 0$), my sample data could easily yield a nonzero estimate. This is again the idea of sampling error which is the recognized difference between parameters and statistics. However, if the true slope is zero, my sample estimate will likely not be *too far* away from zero. The objective in this section is to conduct hypothesis tests using sample data to make a conclusion regarding whether the slope is equal to zero or something different from zero.

The following is the null and alternative hypothesis we wish to test:

$$H_0 : \beta_1 = 0$$
$$H_A : \beta_1 \neq 0$$

Notice the familiar two-tail hypothesis test format. The null states that there is no relationship between X and Y, which implies that X is *insignificant* (i.e., it has an insignificant effect on Y). The alternative hypothesis is that X has a nonzero impact on Y; that is, X is *significant*. Given a chosen level of significance $= \alpha$, there will be a rejection region of size $\alpha/2$ in each tail of the distribution. Since we know that b_1 follows a t-distribution, the tails are symmetric and the critical values depend on the degrees of freedom. With regression, the degrees of freedom are calculated by the number of observations minus the number of estimated parameters. Since with simple linear regression we always estimate two parameters (β_0 and β_1), the degrees of freedom $= n - 2$. With our data, $df = 40 - 2 = 38$. Figure 11.4 illustrates the hypothesis test at the 0.05 level.

To make a conclusion, we have to consider the test statistic. The test statistic is simply calculated by taking the value of b_1 and dividing it by its standard error. Both are included in the regression output in Figure 11.2, but so

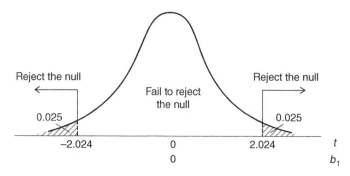

Figure 11.4 Test of significance of the slope at $\alpha = 0.05$.

is the t_{stat}, so there is no need to calculate it by hand; that is $t_{stat} = 4.06$. The interpretation is that the slope estimate of 1.63 is 4.06 standard errors above zero. Since 4.06 is beyond the positive critical t-value of 2.024, we reject the null hypothesis. Rejecting the null indicates that X is significant in explaining changes in Y at the 0.05 level. In other words, attendance is a significant variable in explaining course grades. We can interpret the p-value to illustrate just how significant attendance is. The two-tail p-value, also provided in the output, is 0.0002. Therefore, we reject the null for any significance level greater than 0.0002 suggesting that attendance is highly significant. The table also provides the 95% confidence interval around b_1, which ranges from 0.819 to 2.446. The confidence interval can also be used to complete the hypothesis test at the 0.05 level. Since zero is outside of the interval, we reject the null hypothesis that $\beta_1 = 0$. What is the overarching point? Go to class.

In general, we are not too concerned about testing the significance of the intercept β_0. If we were, however, the procedure is conducted the same way but using b_0 as the sample statistic.

11.6 Goodness of Fit

The regression results strongly suggest that attending class can improve grades in an undergraduate statistics course. However, it is clear from the scatterplot that attendance does not completely explain the performance in the class. In this section, we measure how much of the variation in course grades is explained by variation in attendance. Or more generally, how much of the variation in Y is explained by variation in X. Using a scatterplot as a visual, if all of the points in the scatterplot fell on the fitted regression line, then we would say 100% of the variation in Y is explained by variation in X. In other words, the line is a perfect fit of the data.

The statistic we use to measure how well the regression line fits the data is formally called the *coefficient of determination*, but is most often referred to as r^2. The statistic r^2 reports the fraction of the total variation in a dependent variable that is explained by variation in the independent variable. To really understand r^2, we have to consider the three types of variation in the sample data.

The first is the total variation in the dependent variable Y. The total variation is measured by taking the deviations of every individual value of Y relative to the average value of Y. Those deviations are squared (to put positive and negative deviations in equal footing) and then summed (to get the total). For this reason, the total variation in Y is called the "total sum of squares" and is labeled as (SST), where "SS" indicates the sum of squares.

The total variation in Y is the sum of two other types of variation. One is the variation in Y that is explained by changes in X – called the "regression sum of squares" (SSR) – and the other is the variation in Y that is left unexplained by changes in X – called the "error sum of squares" (SSE). The term "error" here refers to residuals. The accounting relationship is $SST = SSR + SSE$. The term SSE is exactly the term that we minimize when using OLS to estimate the regression line. If $SSE = 0$ it means that every data point is on the regression line and the line is a perfect fit. Clearly, if $SSE = 0$, then $SST = SSR$ which indicates that all the variation in Y is explained by variation in X. The formulas can be found in the Technical Appendix.

Using these three measures, we can form the equation for $r^2 = SSR/SST$. A perfect fit is $r^2 = 1$ which indicates both $SSR = SST$ and $SSE = 0$. In reality, we should never expect a perfect fit of a regression line to the sample of data. The range that r^2 can take is between 0 and 1, and the closer to 1 the better the line fits the data.

All three measures of variation and the calculation of r^2 which can be found in the regression output in Figure 11.2. They are found in the middle section of the output labeled ANOVA, which stands for Analysis of Variance. The column labeled "SS" contains the measures of variation. In our data, $SST = 2250.78$, $SSR = 681.56$, and $SSE = 1569.21$. Therefore, $r^2 = SSR/SST = 0.3028$. r^2 can also be found in the top segment of the regression output. It tells us that 30.28% of the total variation in grades is explained by the variation in the number of classes attended. In other words, about 70% of the differences in grades is not explained by attendance. An r^2 of only 30.28% should not be thought of as "bad." Rather, it just lets us know that there is more to the story about what affects student's grades. We will pick this example back up in the next chapter and add more variables that might help explain more of the variation in grades.

11.7 Checking for Violations of the Assumptions

The assumptions we made about the random error term ε have some important implications concerning our results. Because we do not observe ε, we use the residuals (e's) from our sample of data for clues as to whether the assumptions appear to be violated. For our purposes, we will not consider structured tests of the assumptions, rather, we will conduct simple visual checks. The first assumption we made – that the random errors are on average zero – is imposed when estimating the regression line, so it will always be true. Also, the fourth assumption about the independence of the random errors is primarily a problem with time series data (datasets that track activity over time) and so we do not address it here.

11.7.1 The Normality Assumption

Assumption 2 was that the random errors are distributed normally. This assumption is required to justify the use of the t-distribution when describing

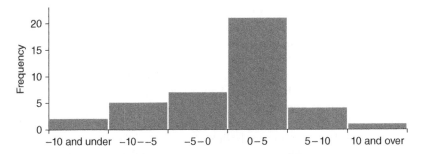

Figure 11.5 Histogram of the 40 residuals for grades and attendance.

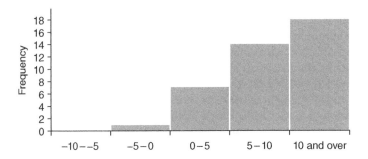

Figure 11.6 A violation of the assumption that the errors are distributed normally (the residuals appear to be left-skewed).

the sampling distribution of b_0 and b_1. If the assumption is violated, our estimates of b_0 and b_1 remain unbiased, but the tests of significance would be suspect. One way to check for normality of the error terms is to create a histogram with all of the residuals. We have 40 observations in our dataset, so we have 40 residuals. The histogram of the residuals will have a mean value of zero (by construction) and it is the shape we are interested in. The more skewed the distribution looks, the more likely we are violating the assumption of normality. Let us take a look at the histogram of our 40 errors.

Looking at Figure 11.5, the shape of the distribution of residuals looks fairly normal. There are no dramatic signs of skewness. The histogram provides a confirmation that our assumption of normality regarding the unobserved errors is not violated. See Figure 11.6 for an example of residuals that appear to violate the assumption of normality.

11.7.2 The Constant Variance Assumption

Assumption 3 was that the random errors have the same variance over all values of X. When the random errors have constant variance, they are homoskedastic, but if this assumption is violated, then the errors are heteroskedastic.

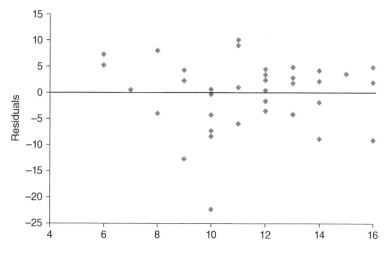

Figure 11.7 Residuals plotted against the number of classes attended.

Heteroskedastic errors do not affect the estimates of β_0 or β_1, and these estimates will remain unbiased. However, if errors are heteroskedastic, then the standard errors will be biased and potentially understated (i.e., too low). When standard errors are lower than they should be, the test statistic is higher than it should be, and we are more likely to reject a null hypothesis. In other words, we might find evidence that a variable is more significant than it should be if the assumption of homoskedasticity is violated.

One way to visually check the integrity of this assumption is to create a scatterplot of the residuals on the vertical axis and the values of the independent variable on the horizontal axis. This is illustrated in Figure 11.7.

The dark horizontal line in Figure 11.7 is the average of the residuals (equal to zero). Observations below the line are negative deviations and observations above the line are positive deviations. We observe variation in the residuals around zero, but no noticeable patterns. A violation would show a noticeable change in the variation in residuals across X. Typical examples include residuals that "fan out" in that the variation increases with increases in X, or residuals that "funnel in" in that the variation decreases with increases in X. See Figure 11.8 for an example of data that suggest heteroskedastic errors.

In our data, there appears to be one large (in absolute terms) residual in comparison to the others. There was a student who attended 10 classes and scored 61 in the class. The student's predicted grade for 10 classes is roughly 83. The residual attached to that student is $e = -22$. Apart from that observation, the data appear to vary around the mean in a constant fashion. This evidence supports the assumption that the errors are homoskedastic. I mean, who does not like homoskedastic errors?

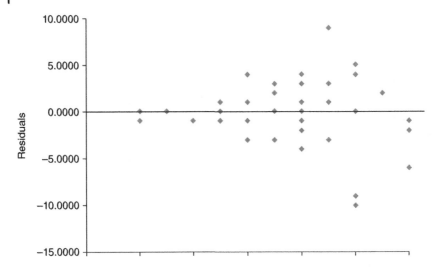

Figure 11.8 A violation of the homoskedasticity assumption that the errors have constant variance (the residuals appear to be heteroskedastic since deviations increase as X increases).

11.8 Summary

This chapter serves as an introduction to linear regression analysis. The term "simple" linear regression is used when we consider only a bivariate (two variable) relationship. Examples include course grades and class attendance, life expectancy and exercise, job performance, and salary. We start with a theory about the relationship between a variable Y that depends on values for X. Hence, Y is the dependent variable and X is the independent variable. The underlying assumption is that the relationship between Y and X takes a linear form. A sample of data is taken and the presumed linear relationship is estimated using a criterion called ordinary least squares. The end result is a line – called the sample regression function – that can be used for a number of purposes. We can use the sample regression results to predict values of Y for given values of X. The results also provide information on the expected change in Y caused by a marginal change in X. Perhaps most importantly, we can use the results to conduct hypothesis tests. The tests inform us of whether the variable X has a significant impact on the variable Y. The fundamentals presented in this chapter will carry over to the next two chapters in which we explore multiple relationships.

Technical Appendix

The *Pearson correlation coefficient* is:

$$r = \frac{\Sigma(X_i - \overline{X})(Y_i - \overline{Y})}{\sqrt{\Sigma(X_i - \overline{X})^2}\sqrt{\Sigma(Y_i - \overline{Y})^2}}, \tag{A.1}$$

where $\overline{X}$ and $\overline{Y}$ denote the mean values for X and Y, respectively. The OLS equation for the slope estimate is

$$b_1 = \frac{\Sigma(X_i - \overline{X})(Y_i - \overline{Y})}{\Sigma(X_i - \overline{X})^2}, \tag{A.2}$$

where b_1 is the estimate of the unknown β_1. The equation to estimate the intercept is

$$b_0 = \overline{Y} - b_1 \overline{X}, \tag{A.3}$$

where b_0 is the estimate of the unknown β_0. When testing the significance of X on Y, the test statistic is

$$t_{\text{stat}} = \frac{b_1 - \beta_1}{s_{b_1}}, \tag{A.4}$$

where s_{b_1} is the standard error. The standard error of the slope estimate is

$$s_{b_1} = \frac{\sqrt{SSE/(n-2)}}{\sqrt{\Sigma(x_i - \overline{x})^2}}. \tag{A.5}$$

The confidence interval for the slope estimate is

$$b_1 \pm t_{\alpha/2} s_{b_1}, \tag{A.6}$$

where $t_{\alpha/2}$ is the critical t-value. The total sum of squares $= SST$ is calculated as:

$$SST = \Sigma(Y_i - \overline{Y})^2. \tag{A.7}$$

The regression sum of squares $= SSR$ is calculated as

$$SSR = \Sigma(\hat{Y}_i - \overline{Y})^2, \tag{A.8}$$

where $\hat{Y}_i$ is the estimate of Y for a given X_i. The error sum of squares $= SSE$ is calculated as

$$SSE = \Sigma(\hat{Y}_i - Y_i)^2. \tag{A.9}$$

The coefficient of determination $= r^2$ is calculated as

$$r^2 = \frac{SSR}{SST} = 1 - \frac{SSE}{SST}. \tag{A.10}$$

12

Multiple Regression

In Chapter 11, we used regression analysis to estimate the relationship between grades and attendance rates. The results suggested that attending more classes will lead to higher grades on average. However, attendance only explained a fraction of the differences observed in students' grades. There must be more to the story. There are of course other variables that may affect the performance, and if we can gather data on those variables, we should include them in our analysis. In this chapter, we analyze regression using multiple independent variables. A simple linear regression is really just a special case of *multiple regression*, and outside of undergraduate classes in statistics they are both just called regression.

In this chapter, we will dig deeper into the question of what affects students' course grades in my undergraduate statistics courses. Some of the additional variables we will include are more continuous in nature, including scholastic aptitude test (SAT) scores, hours spent studying, and a score on a logical thinking test. Other variables will be categorical (or qualitative) in nature, including the gender and year of study. We will discuss the differences in interpretations between continuous and binary data in regression. We will also consider how variables may interact with each other. The overarching objectives are the same from Chapter 11. The goal is to estimate the relationship between grades, and the independent variables then use the results for prediction, tests of significance, and goodness of fit. With multiple independent variables, there are some additional statistics and tests we can analyze, but the process is largely the same.

12.1   Population Regression Model

The first step is to write down a model that captures the assumed relationship between the dependent variable and the independent variables. Because we have multiple X variables, we can refer to them in total as a vector of Xs. In general, we can label the X variables with subscripts from 1 to the number of independent variables included in the model. For example, $X_1, X_2, X_3, ..., X_k$,

A Guide to Business Statistics, First Edition. David M. McEvoy.
© 2018 John Wiley & Sons, Inc. Published 2018 by John Wiley & Sons, Inc.

where k denotes the number of independent variables. In the population regression model below $k = 6$.

$$Y = \beta_0 + \beta_1 X_1 + \beta_2 X_2 + \beta_3 X_3 + \beta_4 X_4 + \beta_5 X_5 + \beta_6 X_6 + \varepsilon$$

However, because we have a lot to keep track of with multiple regression, it often provides clarity to substitute the variable names in the model in place of the Y and X notation. Continuing with our example, suppose we model the relationship between course grades and the other variables as:

$$\text{Grade} = \beta_0 + \beta_1 \text{Attend} + \beta_2 \text{SAT} + \beta_3 \text{Female} + \beta_4 \text{HrsStuding}$$
$$+ \beta_5 \text{Senior} + \beta_6 \text{Logic} + \varepsilon$$

Note that we have dropped the subscript i that indexes each individual. Those subscripts are there implicitly, but we have removed them to simplify the exposition. The β terms (from 1 to 6) are the parameter values that measure the impact each of the variables has on grade (the Y variable). The β_0 term is the constant term and ε is again the random error term. We make the same assumptions about the random errors that we did with simple linear regression; that is, they are distributed normally, independent, with mean zero, and constant variance. However, we will add one more assumption with multiple regressions, which will be addressed a bit later. The variable *Attend* is the attendance rate, *SAT* is the student's SAT score on the combined math and verbal sections, *Female* will capture gender, *HrsStuding* is time spent studying outside of class, *Senior* captures whether the student is a senior, and *Logic* is a test score from a logic exercise.

The parameter values in the population regression model (the Greek letters) are not directly observable. Rather, we must use a sample of data to estimate the values for the β terms. For that, we turn to the sample regression function.

12.2 The Data

The dataset we will use to estimate the population regression model consists of 40 observations ($n = 40$) from a previous statistics course. The dataset is too cumbersome to include in a table, so we will discuss the units of the variables in detail. *Grade* is again measured as the percentage grade out of 100 a student earned in the course. *Attend* is measured by the number of classes attended from 0 to 16, *SAT* score is the combined score ranging from 400 to 1600, *HrsStudying* is the number of hours a student reports studying the material outside of class in an average week, and *Logic* is a score from 0 to 100% on a logical thinking test.

The two variables *Female* and *Senior* are different in the sense that they are categorical variables that follow a binary form. The variable *Female* takes on a value of 1 if the student identifies as female and a value of 0 if the student identifies as male. The variable *Senior* takes a value of 1 if the student is a senior and takes a value of 0 if the student is a junior (note only seniors and juniors take this class). Binary, or qualitative, variables are often called *dummy variables* in regression. The label "dummy" does not imply the variables are stupid or meaningless. The important thing to understand about dummy variables is that are interpreted differently than continuous variables. For example, the parameter estimate for female - β_3 - is the impact on *Grade* from the student being female *relative to* a male student. In general, the parameter attached to a binary variable is the impact on Y of X taking on a value of 1 relative to when X takes on a value of 0.

12.3 Sample Regression Function

The objective is again to use ordinary least squares (OLS) to estimate an equation that "best" fits the data. That equation is chosen by minimizing the sum of the squared deviations from the estimated values of $\hat{Y}$ compared to the actual values of Y for each student. Recall, those deviations are referred to as residuals and are denoted as e's. The estimate of the average relationship between Y and the vector of Xs is called the sample regression function. It will take the form:

$$\hat{Y} = b_0 + b_1X_1 + b_2X_2 + b_3X_3 + b_4X_4 + b_5X_5 + b_6X_6$$

We will again rewrite the equation to include the variable names for clarity. Therefore, the sample regression function is:

$$\hat{Grade} = b_0 + b_1\text{Attend} + b_2\text{SAT} + b_3\text{Female} + b_4\text{HrsStuding}$$
$$+ b_5\text{Senior} + b_6\text{Logic}$$

The calculations of the b's can be made using any statistical software program, and we will use the regression feature of Excel's Analysis Toolpak. The results are shown in Figure 12.1. In comparison to the simple linear regression output from Figure 12.2 in Chapter 11, there are more rows of output in the bottom table. Each row provides statistics for the intercept and the six independent variables.

Using the parameter estimates (labeled "Coefficients" in the output), we can fill in the values for our sample regression function (estimates are rounded to two decimal places):

$$\hat{Grade} = 51.45 + 0.83\text{Attend} + 0.02\text{SAT} + 1.87\text{Female}$$
$$+ 0.15\text{HrsStuding} - 1.44\text{Senior} + 0.08\text{Logic}$$

The sample regression function is the estimate of the average relationship between grades and our explanatory variables. The sign in front of each parameter estimate indicates the direction in which the variable impacts course grades. The only negative sign is attached to the variable *Senior*. This suggests that seniors in the class score lower than students taking the class as juniors. The other variables have a positive influence on course grades. Let us use the sample regression function and the regression output to (1) interpret

(a)

Regression statistics	
Multiple R	0.8910
R square	0.7940
Adjust R square	0.7565
Standard error	3.7487
Observations	40

(b)

ANOVA

	df	SS	MS	F-stat	p-value
Regression	6	1787.03	297.84	21.19	0.0000
Residual	33	463.74	14.05		
Total	39	2250.78			

(c)

	Coefficients	Standard error	t-stat	p-value	Lower 95%	Upper 95%
Intercept	51.4536	7.9080	6.5066	0.0000	35.3648	5.5425
Attend	0.8349	0.2968	2.8130	0.0082	0.2310	1.4387
SAT	0.0164	0.0072	2.2711	0.0298	0.0017	0.0311
Female	1.8710	1.3488	1.3872	0.1747	−0.8731	4.6151
HrsStudying	0.1450	0.1177	1.2316	0.2268	−0.0945	0.3844
Senior	−1.4422	1.2381	−1.1649	0.2524	−3.9611	1.0766
Logic	0.0822	0.0385	2.1380	0.0400	0.0040	0.1605

Figure 12.1 Regression output for course grades as a function of a vector of independent variables.

the individual variables, (2) predict a course grade, (3) test the significance of the independent variables, and (4) determine the overall fit.

12.4   Interpreting the Estimates

Our estimates inform us on how changes in each individual X variable influence Y. For continuous variables, the interpretation is that b is the change in Y caused by a one-unit increase in X. When interpreting changes in individual variables, we always make the assumption that everything else remains unchanged. Or, in Latin *ceteris paribus*.

12.4.1 Attendance

The estimate for *Attend* is $b_1 = 0.83$. For each additional class, a student attends the predicted course grade increases by 0.83 percentage points. You may recall from the previous chapter that the estimate of b_1 was 1.63 when it was the only independent variable. That the estimate of b_1 changes when more variables are included is not shocking. It suggests that the omission of important variables when using simple linear regression was introducing bias to the estimated effect of attendance. In other words, the attendance measure was capturing effects that were at least partially explained by other variables. This issue is called *omitted-variable bias*.

12.4.2 SAT

The estimate for the *SAT* score is $b_2 = 0.02$. This suggests as the SAT score goes up by one point, the predicted course grade goes up by 0.02 percentage points. Since the effect is linear, a 100 point increase in the SAT score would result in a $10 \times 0.02 = 2$ percentage point increase.

12.4.3 Hours Studying

The estimate for *HrsStudying* is $b_4 = 0.15$. For every additional hour, a student spends studying outside of class in a given week, the predicted course grade increases by 0.15 percentage points. We could ask the question how many additional hours of studying would be required to raise the expected course grade by 1 percentage point. To figure this out, we can solve *hours* $\times 0.15 = 1$ to find that a student would need to study 6 and 2/3 more hours per week.

12.4.4 Logic Test

The estimate for *Logic* is $b_6 = 0.08$. For every additional percentage point increase in the logic test score, the predicted course grade increases by 0.08 percentage points.

For the two binary (i.e., dummy) variables, the interpretation is that b is the change in Y when $X = 1$ relative to when $X = 0$.

12.4.5 Female

The estimate for *Female* is $b_3 = 1.87$. The predicted course grade for females is 1.87 percentage points higher than that for male students.

12.4.6 Senior

The estimate for *Senior* is $b_5 = -1.44$. The predicted course grade for seniors is 1.44 percentage points lower than that for juniors.

12.5 Prediction

Using the sample regression function, we can predict a course grade for a student with a given set of characteristics. To illustrate, let us predict an overall course grade for a student named Brad Crispens. Brad is a senior, and he is also a bit lazy. He attended eight classes and studies a shocking 2 hours in a given week. His SAT score was 1000 and he scored a 75 on the logic test. What is Brad's expected course grade? To answer this question, we can just plug in Brad's values into the sample regression function. We get:

$$\hat{\text{Grade}} = 51.45 + 0.83(8) + 0.02(1000) + 1.87(0) + 0.15(2)$$
$$- 1.44(1) + 0.08(75) = 82.95$$

Even with his slacker work ethic, Brad can expect 82.95 in the class. Almost a B. As you can see, I am a pretty easy grader. They do not call me "Gravy Davey" for nothing. Of course, 82.95 is just a point estimate. It is possible to also construct a confidence interval around the estimate of 82.95. Although the formulas differ, the process of constructing confidence intervals around sample statistics and their interpretation is covered in Chapter 7.

12.6 Tests of Significance

Which, if any, of the variables significantly affect course grades? To answer this, we will conduct the same form of hypothesis test used in simple linear regression. Here, however, we have to make one more important assumption. We assume that there is *no multicollinearity* among the independent variables. Multicollinearity describes a situation in which two or more of the independent variables are highly correlated with one another. The assumption is just stated here, but we will investigate it in detail later in this chapter.

To determine whether each individual variable is significant on its own, we test the following:

$$H_0 : \beta_i = 0$$
$$H_A : \beta_i \neq 0,$$

where the subscript i denotes each variable from 1 to 6. The fastest and most general way to make a conclusion to this test is using the p-value provided in the regression output. Recall, if the p-value is less than α, then we reject the null hypothesis. Rejecting the null hypothesis suggests that the variable X has a nonzero effect on Y. In other words, if we reject the null hypothesis, then X is considered a *significant variable*.

In our entire regression, only *Attend* is significant at the 0.01 level (p-value $= 0.008$). At the 0.05 level, *Attend*, *SAT*, and *Logic* are all significant variables in explaining course grades. The other variables are not significant at either the 0.01, 0.05, or 0.10 levels. This means that there is no significant difference between females and males or between seniors or juniors. It also means that studying another hour in a given week has an insignificant effect on grades. The findings suggest that course grades depend on some things that the students have before they even sign up for the class. SAT scores, for instance, are determined before college and the logic test is a general measure of the analytical mindset of the student. However, coming to class also matters. Attendance is something students have direct control of and has proved to be helpful in the data.

12.6.1 Joint Hypothesis Test

Individual tests are nice for sure, but sometimes you just want to put it all on the line. I am talking about testing all the parameters of the model together. I am talking about getting crazy. The null hypothesis is that all the parameters are jointly equal to zero (i.e., all Xs have zero impact on Y). The alternative is that at least one of the parameters is nonzero. For our example, with six independent variables, it can be set up as the following:

$$H_0 : \beta_1 = \beta_2 = \beta_3 = \beta_4 = \beta_5 = \beta_6 = 0$$
$$H_A : \text{At least one of the parameters} \neq 0$$

This test is called a *joint hypothesis test* and is concluded by comparing two measures of variability in the dependent variable. Remember that OLS fits the equation by minimizing the sum of the squared residuals. Also, recall that the sum of the squared residuals is denoted as SSE and can be found in the regression output in the Analysis of Variance (ANOVA) section under the column labeled "SS". SSE is one measure of variation used to make a conclusion to the joint hypothesis test. The better the regression fits the data, the smaller the measure of SSE. And a small SSE implies that the regression variables are doing a good job explaining changes in Y. The measure of the variation in Y explained by the regression variables is labeled SSR – the regression sum of squares. This is also found in the regression output. Now, consider the SSR/SSE ratio. The bigger the ratio, the better our regression is in explaining the observed changes in the dependent variable. The test statistic for the joint hypothesis test (i.e., F_{stat}) is this ratio times a measure for degrees of freedom (see Formula A.1). Since it is a ratio of two variances, it follows an F-distribution (like the one introduced in Chapter 10) and the bigger the F_{stat}, the more likely we are going to reject the null hypothesis. A big F_{stat} indicates that a big fraction of the total variation in Y is explained by the variables we included in our regression. Bigger, in other words, is better.

$F_{stat} = 21.19$ in our regression output. The p-value linked to the F_{stat} is listed directly to the right of it and the p-value $= 0.0000$. Since the p-value equals zero up to four decimal places, we know that we can reject the null hypothesis at any reasonable level of significance. Rejecting the null suggests that our regression equation is significant. In other words, taken collectively, our regression does better at predicting Y than just simply using the average of Y for prediction.

In general, rejecting the null of the joint hypothesis test is a very low bar to cross. It just means that at least one of the variables we included actually matters. Failing to reject the null, on the other hand, would be strong evidence that the regression model is fairly useless in explaining differences in Y values.

12.7 Goodness of Fit

Closely related to the joint hypothesis just described, we can consider the measure of r^2 which tells us what fraction of the variation in Y is explained by changes in the regression variables (as before, $r^2 = SSR/Total\ sum\ of\ squares\ (SST)$). In our results, $r^2 = 0.7940$, so 79.40% of changes in grades are explained by our independent variables. Recall that when we only considered attendance rates in the chapter on simple linear regression $r^2 = 0.3028$. Our multiple regressions do a much better job in explaining why students get different grades. Still, about 20% of the variation in grades is left unexplained.

It is important to note that the estimate of r^2 cannot decrease when including additional variables. It can only go up. The intuition is that adding variables cannot lead to less explanatory power, and it might lead to more. The problem is that if statisticians want to increase measures of r^2, they may be tempted to add a slew of variables just to improve the measure of "fit." To discourage this, we can take a look at a statistic called *adjusted* r^2. which can be found in the regression output in Figure 12.1.

Adjusted r^2 is denoted as r^2_{adj} (see Formula A.2). The adjustment is that the measure of r^2 now includes a penalty (or reduction) for every independent variable included. While r^2 will go up when we include an additional X variable, whether r^2_{adj} goes up or down depends on if the increase in r^2 is bigger than the penalty imposed by increasing the number of variables. The bigger the gap between r^2 and r^2_{adj}, the stronger the signals that there are likely useless predictors to the model. A wide gap suggests that the researcher tried to overfit the model by including variables that likely should not be included.

12.8   Multicollinearity

The additional assumption we made when moving from bivariate to multiple regression is that the X variables are not *too highly* correlated with one another. This was the assumption of *no multicollinearity*. Now, some degree of correlation between your independent variables is expected (and even necessary). Problems arise when variables are so closely tied together that our regression analysis is not able to parse out the individual effects of each variable. And, as it turns out, the individual estimates can be pretty nonsensical in the presence of multicollinearity. When we have multicollinearity we have a violation of the assumption of no multicollinearity.

In the extreme case that two variables are included that are identical (or even perfect linear functions of one another), the regression cannot be estimated and one of the variables will be dropped. Obviously, this is an extreme case but sometimes it is useful to start in the extremes. Now, if two or more variables that are highly but not perfectly correlated are included then the regression can be estimated. This is where we can observe problems. One important point is that the existence of multicollinearity does not affect r^2 the overall measure of fit of the model. It can, however, affect the individual parameter estimates and their standard errors. The parameter estimates could become unstable (switching signs) and the standard errors could be inflated. *Why should we care about inflated standard errors*? Because high-standard errors reduce test statistics and therefore increase p-values. High-standard errors could lead you to determine a variable is insignificant when it really is significant. In fact, one way to diagnose the existence of multicollinearity is if the r^2 value is high but the individual variables are insignificant. Another way to diagnose the problem is to calculate what is called a variance inflation factor (VIF).

12.8.1   Variance Inflation Factor (VIF)

The VIF is a very simple statistic that can indicate how correlated one independent variable is with all the other independent variables. In fact, we can ignore the Y variable completely when talking about the VIF. It is calculated by running additional regressions, but this time, using each of the independent variables as a dependent variable. Crazy I know, but just stick with me. Consider our data on course grades. To get the VIF I would first take one of my variables, say *Attend*, and use this as my dependent variable and regress it on the other five variables (*SAT*, *Female*, *HrsStudying*, *Senior*, *Logic*). My only interest in the regression results would be r^2. r^2 would tell us what percentage of the variation in attendance is explained by the other five variables. The higher the r^2, the higher the degree of collinearity between *Attend* and the other variables. It will not tell us which ones exactly, but if we do this for all six variables we will get a pretty good picture. The *VIF* is actually equal to $1/(1 - r^2)$ using the regression results.

(a)

Regression statistics	
Multiple R	0.7963
R square	0.6340
Adjust R square	0.5802
Standard error	2.1661
Observations	40

(b)

ANOVA

	df	SS	MS	F-stat	p-value
Regression	5	276.37	55.27	11.78	0.0000
Residual	34	159.53	4.69		
Total	39	435.90			

(c)

	Coefficients	Standard error	t-stat	p-value	Lower 95%	Upper 95%
Intercept	0.2674	4.5692	0.0585	0.9537	−9.0183	9.5531
SAT	0.0051	0.0041	1.2502	0.2198	−0.0032	0.0134
Female	0.6514	0.7713	0.8445	0.4043	−0.9161	2.2188
HrsStudying	0.0818	0.0665	1.2296	0.2273	−0.0534	0.2171
Senior	0.8291	0.7011	1.1826	0.2452	−0.5957	2.2540
Logic	0.0605	0.0196	3.0812	0.0041	0.0206	0.1005

Figure 12.2 Regressing attendance on the other independent variables.

Let us explore the calculation of the *VIF* for the variable *Attend*. The regression results are in Figure 12.2.

Note that $r^2 = 0.6340$. Plugging this into the VIF equation $= 1/(1 - 0.6340) = 2.73$. The value of 2.73 is the variance inflation factor for the variable *Attend*. Here is the rule: if the *VIF* is greater than 10, it indicates you have a problem with that variable. Some statisticians use a threshold of 5 instead of 10. In either case, we do not observe a violation of our assumption with *Attend*. In fact, the *VIF*s for all six variables are under 5. This tells me that we have not violated the assumption of no multicollinearity in our dataset. Note that if we use the rule that a *VIF* > 10 indicates multicollinearity in our data, that is equivalent to having r^2 for the regression being 0.90 or higher.

12.8.2 An Example of Violating the Assumption of no Multicollinearity

To highlight the existence of multicollinearity and show how devastating it can be to our parameter estimates, let us use an example dataset on housing prices. Suppose we wanted to estimate how the size of a home (in square feet), the lot size (in acres), and the number of bathrooms affect the price of a home. In general, people are willing to pay more for larger homes, larger lot sizes, and more bathrooms so we might expect our estimates to be positive. We have 30 different homes in our dataset. To get a feel for the data, Table 12.1 shows the data for only six homes where *Price* is the home price in thousands of dollars, *SqFt* is the size of the home in square feet, *Acres* is the lot size in acres, and *Baths* is the number of bathrooms.

Estimating the regression equation yields the results in Figure 12.3. Note that $r^2 = 0.9570$, which means that about 96% of the variation in housing prices is explained by square footage, lot size, and the number of bathrooms. The p-values for each variable are less than 0.10 indicating that each variable significantly explains changes in housing price at the 0.10 significance level. The variables *SqFt* and *Acres* are significant at the 0.01 level. The interpretation of the variable *Baths* is that increasing the number of bathrooms in a home by one results in an increase in the price of the home by $16,024. Overall, the high r^2 and the p-values for the three variables suggest that our variables are explaining most of the differences in prices of homes in our data. In other words, we have a pretty good fit of the data.

Now let us add an additional variable. We also have data on the number of bathroom sinks in each of the 30 homes. While it may seem to be silly to consider such a variable, it is not completely off-the-wall. People like sinks and many bathrooms have more than one sink. The problem is, as we will find out, that the number of bathroom sinks is highly correlated with the number of bathrooms. The two variables are not perfectly correlated however as some

Table 12.1 Housing prices as a function of square footage, lot size, and the number of bathrooms (6 of 30 observations shown).

Price	SqFt	Acres	Baths
505.5	2192	0.4	2.5
784.1	3429	0.6	4.0
649.0	2842	0.4	4.0
689.8	2987	0.5	3.5
709.8	3029	0.5	3.0
590.2	2616	0.5	3.0

(a)

Regression statistics	
Multiple R	0.9783
R square	0.9570
Adjust R square	0.9520
Standard error	20.05
Observations	30

(b)

ANOVA

	df	SS	MS	F-stat	p-value
Regression	5	232715.97	77571.99	192.92	0.0000
Residual	26	10454.37	402.09		
Total	29	243170.34			

(c)

	Coefficients	Standard error	t-stat	p-value	Lower 95%	Upper 95%
Intercept	−27.5742	29.2456	−0.9429	0.3544	−87.6893	32.5408
SqFt	0.1707	0.0148	11.5528	0.0000	0.1403	0.2010
Acres	287.0230	60.8623	4.7159	0.0001	161.9188	412.1272
Baths	16.0236	8.4690	1.8920	0.0697	−1.3848	33.4319

Figure 12.3 Regression results on home prices.

Table 12.2 Housing prices as a function of square footage, lot size, the number of bathrooms, and number of bathroom sinks (6 of 30 observations shown).

Price	SqFt	Acres	Baths	BathSinks
505.5	2192	0.4	2.5	3.0
784.1	3429	0.6	4.0	4.0
649.0	2842	0.4	4.0	4.0
689.8	2987	0.5	3.5	4.0
709.8	3029	0.5	3.0	3.0
590.2	2616	0.5	3.0	3.0

(a)

Regression statistics	
Multiple R	0.9804
R square	0.9612
Adjust R square	0.9549
Standard error	19.4379
Observations	30

(b)

ANOVA

	df	SS	MS	*F*-stat	*p*-value
Regression	4	233724.58	58431.14	154.65	0.0000
Residual	25	9445.76	377.83		
Total	29	243170.34			

(c)

	Coefficients	Standard error	*t*-stat	*p*-value	Lower 95%	Upper 95%
Intercept	−45.9666	30.5027	−1.5070	0.1444	−108.7882	16.8549
SqFt	0.1698	0.0143	11.8517	0.0000	0.1403	0.1994
LotSize	7.4987	1.4638	5.12269	0.0000	4.4839	10.5135
Baths	−11.3593	18.6623	−0.6087	0.5482	−49.7951	27.0765
BathsSinks	26.4340	16.1789	1.6339	0.1148	−6.8871	59.7551

Figure 12.4 Regression results on home prices with a number of bathrooms and a number of bathroom sinks.

bathrooms are half bathrooms (no shower) and some bathrooms have more than one sink, but no bathroom has zero sinks. Table 12.2 has the first six observations of the larger sample with the new variable *BathSinks* included.

Again, estimating the regression yields the results in Figure 12.4 highlight how highly correlated independent variables can influence regression results. First, note that the r^2 measure remains high. This should not be shocking as it is always true that r^2 cannot decrease when more variables are added. Note, however, that the individual variable estimate for *Baths* is very different. Most shocking is that the parameter estimate for *Baths* is now negative, suggesting a reduction in housing prices in response to additional bathrooms. We know that this result is nonsense. What we are observing is multicollinearity reeking havoc on our estimates and causing the parameter estimates to be unstable and switching signs. Also, note that *Baths* is no longer significant at the 0.10 level. This is because multicollinearity has caused the estimate of the standard error to be inflated (high) and thus the test statistic is lower and the *p*-value is bigger. These results show textbook (literally) multicollinearity problems. High r^2, insignificant variables (both *Baths*, and *BathSinks*) and crazy signs on the estimates.

Now, calculating the VIFs for each of the four variables reveals that *Baths* and *BathSinks* are too highly correlated with one another. The VIF for *Baths* is 11.53 and the VIF for *BathSinks* is 10.94. Both exceed 10 and suggest the existence of multicollinearity. Of course, in this case, the obvious implication is to drop the variable *BathSinks*. This example is purposefully simplistic. In reality, it may not be obvious *ex ante* that two or more variables are very highly correlated and in those cases, the VIF may be surprising. Shocking even.

12.9 Summary

In this chapter, we expanded the use of linear regression to allow for multiple independent variables. Along the way, we considered how to include qualitative variables - dummy variables - into the analysis and how to interpret the results. The OLS criterion was used to estimate the regression model and we made one additional assumption to those made in the previous chapter on simple linear regression. That assumption was that the vectors of Xs are not too highly correlated with one another. The assumption is called no multicollinearity. As with simple linear regression, the regression results were used for prediction, tests of significance, and goodness of fit. An additional test - the joint hypothesis test - was introduced to simultaneously test the significance of all of the parameters in the regression model. Finally, we explored how to diagnose problems with multicollinearity in the data.

Technical Appendix

The test statistic for the joint hypothesis test is:

$$F_{stat} = \frac{SSR}{SSE} \left(\frac{n - k - 1}{k} \right), \tag{A.1}$$

where SSR is the regression sum of squares, SSE is the error sum of squares, n is the sample size, and k is the number of independent variables. The formula for the adjusted r^2 is:

$$r^2_{adj} = 1 - \left(\frac{(1 - r^2)(n - 1)}{n - k - 1} \right). \tag{A.2}$$

13

More Topics in Regression

One of the goals for this chapter is to link regression analysis with some of the hypothesis tests we conducted in Chapter 10. In Chapter 10, we compared two parameter values. We will show that the same test we learned for comparing two population means can be implemented using ordinary least squares (OLS) regression. Moreover, we can use regression to compare more than two population means. In most statistics textbooks, there is a dedicated chapter for comparing multiple means that is titled *Analysis of Variance* (ANOVA). The ANOVA chapter spends time walking through a separate testing procedure to compare more than two means. However, the results of that testing procedure are fully contained in the ANOVA section of the regression output produced by any statistical software program. In this way, the chapter on ANOVA is usually a bit awkward because the regression techniques learned in the regression chapter cover ANOVA plus much more. Part of this chapter will walk through the process of using the ANOVA section in regression to conduct hypothesis tests of multiple means.

We will also take a brief look at other regression topics covered in some business statistics courses. We will explore how to use OLS regression to estimate relationships that are not predicted to be linear. The chapter also explores how to estimate and interpret the interactions between independent variables. Finally, we will comment on time-series regression and forecasting.

13.1 Hypothesis Tests Comparing Two Means With Regression

Think back to Chapter 10 where Derek Hamburger wanted to test whether the average starting salary was different between economics and accounting majors. The data were provided in Table 10.1 and he had a sample of 35 economics majors and 40 accounting majors. In that chapter, we compared the two average salaries using a two sample t test. Our goal in this section is to use

A Guide to Business Statistics, First Edition. David M. McEvoy.

the regression tool to conduct the same hypothesis test. We will show that our conclusion using the regression tool – relying on the OLS criterion – is identical to the conclusions we made using the two-sample t test.

To begin, we have to format the dataset a bit differently. We are going to stack all of the salaries together in one column (our dependent variable) and then use a dummy variable to indicate whether the salary is from an economics or accounting major (no double majors in this study). In total, there will be $35 + 40 = 75$ observations on salary. In Table 13.1, we include just a subset of the sample to illustrate how the dummy variable is used without taking up too much space. In Table 13.1, the variable *economics* is a dummy variable that takes on a value of "1" when the student earned an economics degree and a "0" when the student studied accounting.

Note that although there are two majors, only one dummy variable is required. This is because one dummy variable provides all the information needed and if we tried to include another variable *accounting* the regression could not be estimated with both included (in fact, most software programs would just drop one of them). The variable *salary* is the dependent variable and *economics* is the single independent variable. Once again, using the regression tool in Excel on the full sample of 75 observations yields the output in Figure 13.1.

The most important pieces of information are t_{stat} for the variable *economics* and its corresponding p-value. Note that $t_{stat} = 2.6019$ and p-value $= 0.0112$, which are the exact results we found in Figure 10.2 in Chapter 10 in which we conducted a two-sample t-test assuming equal variances of the population. Therefore, whenever a regression is used in this way, the underlying assumption

Table 13.1 Starting salaries of economics and accounting majors using a dummy variable (10 of 75 observations).

Salary	Economics
32,897	0
33,283	1
33,899	0
33,978	0
34,388	0
34,665	0
34,679	0
34,740	1
34,767	0
35,025	0

is that the variance in the dependent variable (in our example *salary*) is the same for both populations (in our example economics and accounting majors). It is also useful to understand how to interpret the parameter estimates. The intercept in this simple regression is the average starting salary for accounting majors (where *economics*=0), which is $41,895.28. The estimate of $4991.90 attached to the variable *economics* is the difference in starting salaries between the two majors. That difference in salaries is significantly different from zero at the 0.0112 significance level (i.e., the *p*-value). Just as we concluded before, economics majors earn about $5000 dollars more than accounting majors in starting salaries.

Finally, it is worth pointing out some of the statistics in the ANOVA section of the regression output in Figure 13.1. Notice that the *p*-value that corresponds to the F_{stat} is 0.0112, which is the same as the *p*-value for the t_{stat} for the *economics* variable. When we have only one independent variable, this will always be the

(a)

Regression statistics	
Multiple R	0.2913
R square	0.0849
Adjust R square	0.0723
Standard error	8289.0320
Observations	75

(b)

ANOVA

	df	SS	MS	F-stat	p-value
Regression	1	465155225.80	465155225.80	6.7700	0.0112
Residual	73	5015687780.95	68708051.79		
Total	74	5480843006.75			

(c)

	Coefficients	Standard error	t-stat	p-value	Lower 95%	Upper 95%
Intercept	41895.28	1310.61	31.9662	0.0000	39283.2310	44507.3190
Economics	4991.90	1918.54	2.6019	0.0112	1168.2555	8815.5374

Figure 13.1 Comparing average starting salaries between economics and accounting majors using regression.

case. In fact, $F_{stat} = 6.77$ is simply the t_{stat} squared. The ANOVA section of the regression output is going to play a bigger role in the next section in which we conduct hypothesis tests comparing more than two means. In general, F_{stat} in the ANOVA section is the test statistic for the null hypothesis that all of the independent variables have zero effect on the dependent variable.

13.2 Hypothesis Tests Comparing More Than Two Means (ANOVA)

In this section, we will shed light on one of the most important questions humanity has ever faced. Does the average Grade Point Average (GPA) differ among *geeks*, *dweebs*, and *nerds* during their freshman year in college? Of course, we could spend an entire 200 pages debating the definitions of each, but for our purposes, we will assume that each student in our dataset fits into one category and only one category. In other words, geeks, dweebs, and nerds are mutually exclusive (note that the term "mutually exclusive" is pretty nerdy). We want to conduct a hypothesis test to jointly compare the three means. The null hypothesis is that the average GPAs for all three types are equal. That is, $H_0 : \mu_g = \mu_d = \mu_n$ and the alternative hypothesis is that at least one is different from another.

We can use regression to conduct such a test. Our dataset will have one column of GPAs for all students in the sample and then dummy variables to indicate whether each student is a geek, dweeb, or nerd. There are 50 observations in the dataset, and a subset of 10 observations is included in Table 13.2 to provide a feel for the data. Since there are three categories of students, we

Table 13.2 GPAs for a sample of geeks, dweebs, and nerds (10 of 50 observations shown).

GPA	dweeb	nerd
3.88	0	1
3.88	0	0
3.79	0	1
3.77	1	0
3.74	0	0
3.74	1	0
3.72	0	0
3.60	1	0
3.59	1	0
3.59	0	1

will need $3-1 = 2$ dummy variables. This is always the rule. Given the number of mutually exclusive categories, you will need # of categories - 1 dummy variables.

The first column of data is the student's GPA, which is the dependent variable. The variables *dweeb* and *nerd* are dummy variables (independent variables). We do not include a variable for geeks because whenever there are zeros for both the variables *dweeb* and *nerd* that indicates the student is a geek. That is why a third dummy variable would be redundant and including it would prevent us from estimating the regression. For example, the second student in the dataset in Table 13.2 is a geek with a GPA of 3.88. The first student, of course, is a nerd.

The regression model we are estimating takes the following form (in expected value):

$$E[GPA] = \beta_0 + \beta_1 \text{dweeb} + \beta_2 \text{nerd}.$$

The term β_1 captures the difference in the average GPA for a *dweeb* relative to a geek (the category we omitted). Likewise, the term β_2 captures the difference in the average GPA for a *nerd* relative to a geek. The intercept β_0 will be the average GPA for geeks. The regression results are shown in Figure 13.2.

In order to jointly test the average GPA for all three student types, we form the following null and alternative hypotheses:

$H_0:$ $\beta_1 = \beta_2 = 0$

$H_A:$ At least one of the parameters $\neq 0$

If both β terms are equal to zero (as in the null hypothesis), it means that geeks, dweebs, and nerds all have the same average GPAs. Therefore, if we fail to reject the null, then we can conclude that the average GPA is the same for all three student types. Rejecting the null, on the other hand, simply suggests that at least one of the β terms is nonzero.

The statistics for the joint hypothesis test are contained in the ANOVA section of the regression output in Figure 13.2. The F_{stat} is the ratio of two types of variability. The numerator is the variance in GPAs between student types (geeks, dweebs, and nerds) and the denominator is the variance within each student type. The bigger the F_{stat}, the bigger the variance in GPAs between geeks, dweebs, and nerds relative to the variance within each category. $F_{stat} = 0.2493$ for our data with a corresponding p-value $= 0.7804$. Since the p-value is greater than any reasonable level of significance (1%, 5%, or 10%), we clearly fail to reject the null hypothesis. Thus, we find that the average GPA is equivalent for geeks, dweebs, and nerds. From the bottom table of Figure 13.2, we observe that the individual variable estimates for *dweeb* and *nerd* are also insignificant (p-values of 0.7950 and 0.4911, respectively). This is unsurprising. Failing to reject the joint hypothesis from the ANOVA section

Regression statistics	
Multiple R	0.1025
R square	0.0105
Adjust R square	−0.0316
Standard error	0.7907
Observations	50

ANOVA

	df	SS	MS	F-stat	p-value
Regression	2	0.3117	0.1558	0.2493	0.7804
Residual	47	29.3836	0.6252		
Total	49	29.6953			

	Coefficients	Standard error	t-stat	p-value	Lower 95%	Upper 95%
Intercept	2.8017	0.2042	13.7236	0.0000	2.3910	3.2124
dweeb	−0.0706	0.2701	−0.2613	0.7950	−0.6139	0.4727
nerd	−0.2004	0.2887	−0.6941	0.4911	−0.7812	0.3804

Figure 13.2 Comparing average starting salaries using regression.

suggests that none of the variables significantly influence the values for the dependent variable.

Given the available data, this approach can be used to jointly test any number of population means. Remember that the null hypothesis is that all of the parameters are equal to zero. If you can fail to reject the null that provides quite a bit of information because you know that there is no difference between categories. However, if you reject the null hypothesis, it only suggests that at least one parameter is not equal to zero. In those cases, you want to refer to the individual variable estimates and p-values to discover which variables are significant.

13.3 Interacting Variables

In some cases, we may expect that the interaction of two or more variables may influence a dependent variable. Consider a dataset that attempts to estimate the extent of gender discrimination in the labor market. Suppose, we hypothesize that wages paid for a job depend on the worker's level of experience and his or her gender. We could estimate the following model:

$$E[Wage] = \beta_0 + \beta_1 \text{Experience} + \beta_2 \text{Female}.$$

The variable *Experience* is the number of years of experience in the job and the variable *Female* is a dummy variable that equals one if the worker is a female (and zero if the worker is a male). In this model, β_1 captures the change in wage from an additional year of experience and β_2 captures the difference in wages between males and females given the same level of experience. This model could be used to estimate wage discrimination in terms of starting salaries (when *Experience*=0) for both men and women. If this form of wage discrimination exists, then $\beta_2 < 0$ and it is significant.

However, it is also possible that there is an additional form of gender-driven wage discrimination in the labor market. Female workers may not only start earning less money than men in the same profession, but they also may earn less than men for each additional year of experience. To get at this question, we need to interact *Experience* with *Female*. To create this *interaction variable*, we multiply the two variables together to form *ExpFemale*. With observations for male workers *ExpFemale* = 0 and for female workers *ExpFemale* = *Experience*. The new model takes the following form:

$$E[Wage] = \beta_0 + \beta_1 \text{Experience} + \beta_2 \text{Female} + \beta_3 \text{ExpFemale}.$$

With this model, the change in wage from an additional year of experience for men is β_1. However, the change in wage for an additional year of experience for women is $\beta_1 + \beta_3$. The parameter β_3 can be interpreted as the difference in what women are paid for each additional year of experience relative to men. Again, if $\beta_3 < 0$ and significant, then we can conclude that there is gender-driven wage discrimination in the labor market based on experience.

To estimate the model, we have a sample dataset of 35 observations. The dependent variable *Wage* is in thousands of dollars and ranges from 22 to 114. The variable *Experience* ranges from 0 to 10 years and there is a mix of male and female workers. The regression output is shown in Figure 13.3.

Let us first examine some of the results for the overall fit of the regression model. An $r^2 = 0.9311$ tells us that about 93% of the variation in wages is explained by experience, gender, and the interaction of the two. $F_{stat} = 139.59$ and p-value= 0.0000 tell us that we can reject the null that $\beta_1 = \beta_2 = \beta_3 = 0$.

13.3.1 Gender Differences in Starting Wages

Focusing on the estimates for the individual variables, males with zero years of experience are expected to earn $33,014 (i.e., the value for b_0). Females, on the other hand, are expected to earn $14,147 less than males given zero years of experience (i.e., the starting wage for females is $b_0 + b_2 = \$33,014 -$

Regression statistics	
Multiple R	0.9649
R square	0.9311
Adjust R square	0.9244
Standard error	8.0612
Observations	35

ANOVA

	df	SS	MS	F-stat	p-value
Regression	3	27213.43	9071.14	139.59	0.0000
Residual	31	2014.46	64.98		
Total	34	29227.89			

	Coefficients	Standard error	t-stat	p-value	Lower 95%	Upper 95%
Intercept	33.0138	4.1556	7.9445	0.0000	24.5385	41.4892
Exp	8.6106	0.7065	12.1882	0.0000	7.1697	10.0515
Female	−14.1467	5.8174	−2.4318	0.0210	−26.0114	−2.2820
Femaleexp	−5.1459	1.0225	−5.0328	0.0000	−7.2313	−3.0605

Figure 13.3 Wage as a function of experience and gender.

$14,147 = \$18,867$). Since the p-value $= 0.0210$ for b_2, we can say that this difference in starting wage amounts is significant at the 0.025 level and above.

13.3.2 Gender Differences in Wage Increase from Experience

For each additional year of experience, males are expected to increase their wage by $b_1 = \$8611$, which is highly significant with a p-value $= 0.0000$. The estimated change in wage for an additional year of experience for females is $b_1 + b_3 = \$8611 - \$5146 = \$3465$. Therefore, males earn $5146 more than females for each additional year of experience. The p-value for b_3 is 0.0000 and therefore this difference is significant.

Both the dummy variable for gender and the interaction term illustrate that there is gender-based wage discrimination in the labor market. Females start with lower salaries and then earn less for each additional year of experience. Figure 13.4 illustrates the wage differences from the regression. The top line is the sample regression function for males (plug 0 in for *Female*) and the bottom

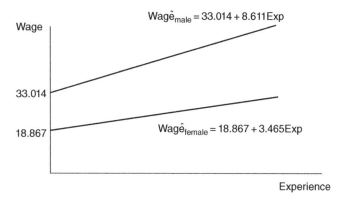

Figure 13.4 Sample regression functions for both males and females.

line is the sample regression function for females. The starting points are different and so are the slopes. The gender wage gap increases with every additional year of experience.

In general, interaction variables are constructed by multiplying one variable by another. While it is possible to create interaction variables by combining three or more variables, the interpretation of the results quickly becomes very difficult.

13.4 Nonlinearities

Over the past few chapters have used the OLS criterion to estimate linear regression models. Even with multiple independent variables, the implicit assumption is that the models we estimate are *linear in the parameters.* In all the cases we have considered thus far, a one-unit change in the variable X is expected to have the same impact on Y over the entire range of X values. While this may be true for some relationships, it may not be true for others. Consider the relationship between the exam grade (a dependent variable) and study time (the independent variable). For most students, studying is beneficial and the expectation is that the hours spent studying will have a positive effect on exam grades. However, there comes a point where additional hours studying do not have the same impact on performance. This is the idea of diminishing marginal productivity of studying. The first few hours may have a big payoff, but the last few hours may have little impact or could even have a negative impact (e.g., lack of sleep decreases the performance).

As another example, consider the impact increasing carbon emissions has on the average temperature of the earth. Most scientists agree that an increase in carbon emissions causes an increase in average temperature. They also predict that the marginal increase in temperature intensifies as carbon emissions increase. In this case, there is an increasing marginal impact of carbon emissions on temperature.

It is possible to use OLS to estimate these types of nonlinear relationships between Y and X. We can achieve this by adding a squared term as an additional independent variable. The regression equation would then take a *quadratic form*. Consider the following bivariate relationship between Y and X.

$$E[Y] = \beta_0 + \beta_1 X + \beta_2 X^2$$

The squared term is the simple calculation of $X \times X$. The term β_2 captures potential changes in X's marginal influence on Y for larger values of X. The important point now is that the estimated change in Y caused by a one-unit increase in X is not β_1, but $\beta_1 + 2X$.[1] With this specification, the size of the change in Y caused by a one-unit increase in X depends on the reference value for X. In other words, the relationship between Y and X is nonlinear if $\beta_2 \neq 0$.

The most important thing is interpreting the signs on the parameter estimates for β_1 and β_2. Note that if $\beta_2 = 0$, then we are back to the linear relationship between Y and X. When $\beta_2 \neq 0$, there are four possibilities we need to consider regarding the combined signs for β_1 and β_2. They are illustrated in Figure 13.5.

The upper-left quadrant (a) of Figure 13.5 illustrates a case of increasing marginal influence of X on Y. Higher levels of X cause more dramatic changes in Y. The graph in (a) could represent the example of carbon emissions on temperature: higher levels of carbon have more devastating incremental impacts on average temperatures. The graph in the upper-right quadrant (b) illustrates the case of decreasing marginal productivity. We discussed the case of studying for exams as an example of such nonlinearity between X and Y. Studying leads to improvements in average grades until a point in which more studying has perverse effects. The graph in quadrant (c) shows an initial negative relationship between X and Y that turns positive with larger values for X. An example of this could be an average cost curve as a function of output for a firm. A firm's average cost decreases with initial increases in output because marginal costs are low and fixed costs do not change. However, as the marginal costs increase with production so does the average cost curve. The graph in quadrant (d) shows X having a negative effect on Y and that the negative effect intensifies with larger values for X. This graph could represent the impact drug use has on long-term memory. Relatively low levels of drug use reduce long-term memory and that memory loss is exacerbated with increases in drug use. Again, in the reference case in which $\beta_2 = 0$, the relationship between X and Y is the familiar straight line.

---

[1] The term $\beta_1 + 2X$ is found by taking the partial derivative of $E[Y] = \beta_0 + \beta_1 X + \beta_2 X^2$ with respect to X.

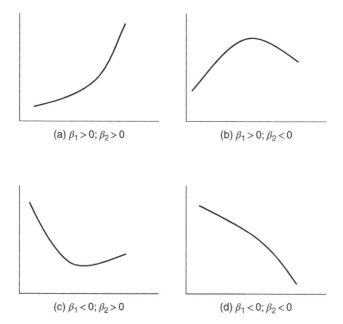

(a) $\beta_1 > 0; \beta_2 > 0$

(b) $\beta_1 > 0; \beta_2 < 0$

(c) $\beta_1 < 0; \beta_2 > 0$

(d) $\beta_1 < 0; \beta_2 < 0$

Figure 13.5 Potential nonlinear relationships between expected Y (vertical axes) and X (horizontal axes).

13.5 Time-Series Analysis

Most of the datasets we have worked with in this book are cross-sectional in nature. Cross-sectional data consist of many observations gathered from one point in time. In that sense, there is no obvious order or sequence to the data. Student course grades from a statistics class in a given semester are an example of cross-sectional data. Time-series data, on the other hand, consist of observations spanning over different points in time. These data have a natural chronological order. An example of time-series data would be measures of attendance taken for each class period over the entire semester. You may be shocked to learn that attendance in my business statistics course is not 100%. Even more shocking is that the data show a trend in which attendance rates fall as the semester drags on (with the predicable spike on review days before exams). Fitting trend is often an important goal of analyzing time-series data. Investors often follow a company's stock price over time to get a feel for performance and perhaps to forecast into the near future. Climate scientists pour over time-series data on average temperatures and carbon emissions to try and isolate a causal relationship. Measures of economic well-being (e.g., Gross Domestic Product (GDP)) and standard of living are tracked over time to provide an indication of whether or not we are making progress.

Time-series analysis is really a topic that can stand alone as part of undergraduate course in business and economics. There are many different approaches to fitting time trends and understanding temporal relationships between variables. The objective in this section is just to highlight how we can use the linear regression techniques covered over the past few chapters to fit trend lines to time-series data and how these can be used in forecasting.

Let us consider time-series data on world records for women's long jump. World records for women's long jump date back to 1922. [2] Figure 13.6 is a scatterplot of women's long jump world records in meters from 1922–1988.

Looking at the progression of data over time in Figure 13.6, it is clear that the data suggest a linear trend. We can fit a trend line using OLS regression. The line chosen using OLS will be the one that minimizes the sum of the squared deviations from the line. The data lead to the following sample regression function

$$\hat{\text{Meters}} = 4.6894 + 0.031\,\text{Year}$$

where *Year* equals 0 for the year 1900 and increases by one for every year after 1900. For example, using the regression line to predict the world record in 1985 would result in $4.6894 + 0.031(85) = 7.32$ meters (in reality, it was 7.44 meters). The trend line fits the data very well. Using r^2 as a measure of overall fit, we get $r^2 = 0.9652$. With $r^2 = 1$ being a perfect fit, I would say the linear trend line fits the data extremely well.

With such a clearly defined trend, it is tempting to forecast women's long jump world records into the future. While there is no harm in experimenting, we must be careful about how much weight we put in these results. If a new world record in women's long jump will be recorded at the next summer Olympics in 2020, our model would predict that record would be set at 8.41

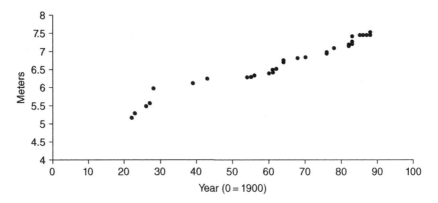

Figure 13.6 Women's long jump world records.

---

2 The Federation Sportive Feminine Internationale (FSFI) maintained records from 1922 up to 1936 when it was absorbed by the International Association of Athletics Federations (IAAF).

meters (plug in 120 for *Year*). Of course, this forecast is made assuming the linear trend continues. Perhaps it will. But, considering that the model would also suggest that the women's long jump record was 0 meters back in 1749, we should remain suspect of persistent linear trends.

13.6 Summary

This chapter concludes the material on linear regression analysis. One goal was to link regression results to the two sample *t* tests we explored in Chapter 10 and then to demonstrate that regression can be used to conduct hypothesis tests comparing more than two means. That is, linear regression can be used to achieve the same goals as single-factor ANOVA. We also explored the use of interaction variables and how to use linear regression to estimate potential nonlinearities in the data. We concluded by discussing the use of linear trend lines in time-series data and forecasting.

Index

F distribution   127, 155
F-stat for folded F test   131
F-stat for joint hypothesis test   163, 169
F-test   127, 155
p-value   99, 101, 108, 132, 142, 154, 156, 157, 159, 166, 171
p-value rule   99, 108, 155
r^2 142, 147, 156
t distribution   76, 78, 91, 93, 120, 141
t-stat for b_1 147
t-stat for a mean σ unknown   101
t-stat for a mean   101
t-table   85, 87, 96, 142
t-test assuming equal variances   121, 131
t-test assuming unequal variances   122, 131
t-test for a mean with dependent samples   125
t-test for a mean with paired observations   131
z distribution   46–48, 50
z-score for a mean   71
z-score for a proportion   72
z-score for binomial x 51, 52
z-score for continuous x 46, 52
z-stat for a mean σ known   101
z-stat for a proportion   107, 115
z-stat for two proportions   132
z-table   46, 53, 54, 67, 76, 85, 107
ceteris paribus   153

a
abnormal errors   144
adjusted r^2 156, 163
alternative hypothesis   92
Analysis Toolpak in Excel   137, 151
ANOVA   143, 165, 167

b
bell-shaped distribution   43
Bernoulli trials   49
binary data   2, 49, 103
binomial distribution   49, 52, 68, 80, 85
bivariate   133

c
categorical data   2, 48, 103, 109, 111
categorical variables   149, 150
Central Limit Theorem   62, 66, 75, 91
chance   31
Chebyshev's theorem   28, 44
chi-square test of goodness of fit   111
chi-square test of independence   109
chi-square test statistic   115
chi-square tests   104
cluster sampling   16
coding data   2
coefficient of determination   142, 147

A Guide to Business Statistics, First Edition. David M. McEvoy.
© 2018 John Wiley & Sons, Inc. Published 2018 by John Wiley & Sons, Inc.

combination formula   56, 71
Complement Rule   42
conditional probabilities   32, 38
conditional probability formula   42
confidence interval for a mean   74
confidence interval for a proportion
   86
confidence interval for mean σ known
   85
confidence interval for mean σ
   unknown   85
confidence intervals   73
confidence level   76
contingency table   37, 40, 109, 110,
   115
continuous probability distributions
   43
continuous variables   3, 48, 80, 151
convenience sample   16, 75
critical F-value   127, 132
critical t-value   79, 87, 142
critical t-value simple linear regression
   147
critical value   76, 94
cross-sectional data   5
cumulative standard normal table   47,
   53, 54

d

degrees of freedom   25, 30, 79
degrees of freedom for simple linear
   regression   141
dependent events   33
dependent samples   125, 131
dependent variable   134
discrete variables   3
distribution-free tests   109
dummy variables   151, 166

e

empirical probabilities   37
Empirical Rule   44, 45, 48, 67, 76, 93,
   96, 130

error sum of squares – *SSE*   143, 147
event   32
expected value   49
experiments   16
explanatory variable   134

f

finite population correction factor   65,
   66, 71, 72
Folded F-test   127
forecasting with a linear trend   176
frequency   26

g

Gaussian   43
General Law of Addition   42
General Law of Multiplication   42
goodness of fit   142, 156
Gravy Davey   154

h

heteroskedasticity   140, 144, 145
histogram   26, 43, 55, 57, 59, 64
homoskedasticity   140, 144
hypergeometric distribution   69
hypothesis tests of two means   117,
   118
hypothesis tests of two proportions
   117, 128
hypothesis tests of two variances   117,
   126

i

independent events   33
independent samples   118
independent variable   134
inferential statistics   10, 61
interaction variables   171
intercept estimate   147
intersections   36, 42
interval data   5

j

joint hypothesis test   155, 163, 169

k
K.A.C. Manderville   55
Karl Gauss   43

l
left-skewed   27, 66
level of measurement   4
level of significance   78, 94
likelihood   31
line chart   6

m
margin of error   73, 77
margin of error comparing two
    proportions   83
margin of error for a mean σ known
    85
margin of error for mean σ unknown
    85
margin of error for the difference in
    two proportions   83, 86
mean   20
mean absolute deviation   25, 29
measures of central tendency   20
median   23
mode   24
mound-shaped distribution   43
multicollinearity   154, 157
multiple dummy variables   169
multiple regression   149
mutually exclusive   34

n
nominal data   4
nonresponse bias   15
normal approximation of a binomial
    distribution   50, 52, 68, 71, 85,
    104, 115
normal distribution   43–45, 47
null hypothesis   92
numerical data   3

o
omitted variables   134
omitted-variable bias   153
one-tail hypothesis test of a mean   97
one-tail hypothesis test of a proportion
    107
ordinal data   4
ordinary least squares   137, 151, 166,
    173, 176

p
Pafnuty Chebyshev   28
panel data   7
Pearson correlation coefficient   137,
    147
percentile   23
pooled variance   121, 131
population   9
population mean   21, 29
population parameter   13, 21
population proportion   67
population regression model   134, 149
population standard deviation   25, 29
population variance   25, 29
power   124
prediction   139
probability   31
proportion   67, 103

q
quadratic form   174
qualitative data   2
qualitative variables   150
quantitative data   3

r
random number generator   12
range   24
ratio data   5
regression   133, 149, 165
regression sum of squares – *SSR*   142,
    147
rejection region   94, 106
relative frequency   37, 43, 57, 58

residual   137
right-skewed   26
Ronald Fisher   127

s
sample   11
sample mean   22, 29, 30, 57, 61
sample proportion   67, 115
sample regression function   135, 151
sample standard deviation   26, 30
sample statistic   13
sample variance   25, 30
sample weights   15
sampling bias   11
sampling distribution of a mean   58
sampling distribution of a proportion   67
sampling distributions   55
sampling error   13, 57, 67, 93, 141
sampling with replacement   12, 33, 104
sampling without replacement   12, 33, 62
scatterplot   135
self-report   16
simple linear regression   133
simple probabilities   32
simple random sampling   11
skewed data   26
slope estimate   147
smallest sample size required   86
Special Law of Addition   42
Special Law of Multiplication   42
standard deviation of a binomial distribution   52
standard error   64
standard error of a mean   66, 71, 75, 91
standard error of a proportion   68, 71, 85, 105, 115
standard normal distribution   46

standard normal table   46
standardizing data   52
statistics   1
strata   14
stratified sampling   14
Student's *t*-distribution   76
surveys   16
symmetric data   26
systematic sampling   15

t
tests of significance   154
Theo Epstein   xiii
time-series analysis   175
time-series data   5
total sum of squares - *SST*   142, 147
trials   49
two-tail hypothesis test of a mean   92
two-tail hypothesis test of a proportion   104
Type I error   93
Type I error probability   94
Type II error   93, 96
Type II error probability   96

u
unbiased estimate   62, 68, 140
union   35, 42
unstable estimates   162

v
variance   24
variance inflation factor rule   158
variation inflation factor   157
Venn diagram   37
violations of regression assumptions   143

w
Welch–Satterthwaite degrees of freedom   123, 131

Printed and bound by CPI Group (UK) Ltd, Croydon, CR0 4YY

16/04/2025

14658456-0002